Mathematics Olympiad

Highly useful for all school students participating
in Various Olympiads & Competitions

Series Editor Keshav Mohan
Author Sanjeev Kumar

Class 8

arihant

ARIHANT PRAKASHAN, MEERUT

ARIHANT PRAKASHAN, MEERUT
All Rights Reserved

卐 **Administrative & Production Offices**

Corporate Office	'Ramchhaya' 4577/15, Agarwal Road, Darya Ganj New Delhi -110002 Tele: 011- 47630600, 43518550; Fax: 011- 23280316
Head Office	Kalindi, TP Nagar, Meerut (UP) - 250002 Tele: 0121-2401479, 2512970, 4004199; Fax: 0121-2401648

All disputes subject to Meerut (UP) jurisdiction only.

卐 **Sales & Support Offices**

Agra, Ahmedabad, Bengaluru, Bhubaneswar, Bareilly, Chennai, Delhi, Guwahati, Haldwani, Hyderabad, Jaipur, Jalandhar, Jhansi, Kolkata, Kota, Lucknow, Meerut, Nagpur & Pune

卐 **ISBN**   978-93-5203-395-9

卐 **Price**   ₹75

Typeset by Arihant DTP Unit at Meerut

Printed & Bound by Arihant Publications (I) Ltd. (Press Unit)

Production Team

Publishing Manager	Mahendra Singh Rawat	*Page Layouting*	Diwakar Gaur
Project Head	Karishma Yadav	*DTP Operator*	Akash
Project Coordinator	Divya Gusain	*Cover Designer*	Syed Darin Zaidi
Proof Reader	Reena Garg	*Inner Designer*	Deepak Kumar

For further information about the products from Arihant
log on to www.arihantbooks.com or email to info@arihantbooks.com

Preface

Mathematics Olympiad Series for Class 6th -10th is a series of books which will challenge the young inquisitive minds by the non-routine and exciting mathematical problems.

The main purpose of this series is to make the students ready for competitive exams. The school/board exams are of qualifying nature but not competitive, they do not help the students to prepare for competitive exams, which mainly have objective questions.

- **Need of Olympiad Series**
  This series will fill this gap between the School/Board and Competitive Exams as this series have all questions in Objective format. This series helps students who are willing to sharpen their problem solving skills. Unlike typical assessment books, which emphasis on drilling practice, the focus of this series is on practicing problem solving techniques.

- **Development of Logical Approach**
  The thought provoking questions given in this series will help students to attain a deeper understanding of the concepts and through which students will be able to impart reasoning/Logical/Analytical skills in them.

- **Complement Your School Studies**
  This series complements the additional preparation needs of students for regular school/board exams. Along with, it will also address all the requirements of the students who are approaching National/State level competitions or Olympiads.

We shall welcome criticism from the students, teachers, educators and parents. We shall also like to hear from all of you about errors and deficiencies, which may have remained in this edition and the suggestions for the next edition.

Editor & Author

Contents

1

Rational Number

1. A rational number, which is less than every positive real number and greater than every negative rational number, is
   - a -1
   - b 1
   - c Can't say
   - d 0

2. $\left(\frac{2}{5} + \frac{15}{25} - 5\right) + \left(\frac{7}{15}\right)$ is equal to
   - a $\frac{53}{15}$
   - b $\frac{1}{15}$
   - c $-\frac{53}{15}$
   - d $-\frac{1}{15}$

3. Which of the following rational numbers has no reciprocal?
   - a $\frac{3}{5}$
   - b $\frac{7}{9}$
   - c 0
   - d $\frac{5}{9}$

4. Which one of the following is a natural number?
   - a $\frac{15}{60}$
   - b $\frac{17}{51}$
   - c $\frac{81}{27}$
   - d $\frac{25}{35}$

5. In the given figure,

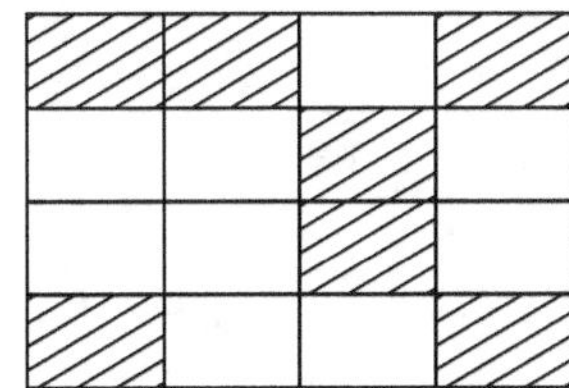

   The shaded area can be represented as the fraction of whole figure in $\frac{p}{q}$ form. The fraction will be
   - a $\frac{1}{2}$
   - b $\frac{8}{16}$
   - c $\frac{7}{16}$
   - d $\frac{8}{15}$

6. The sum of two rational numbers is (-3). If one of them is $\left(-\frac{6}{7}\right)$. Then, other number is
   - a $\frac{15}{7}$
   - b $-\frac{15}{7}$
   - c $\frac{27}{7}$
   - d $-\frac{27}{7}$

7. Dividing the sum of $\frac{77}{14}$ and $\frac{195}{26}$ by their difference, we get the positive number as
   - a $\frac{4}{26}$
   - b $\frac{38}{6}$
   - c $\frac{91}{14}$
   - d None of these

8. If $a = \frac{1}{5}$, then the value of $\left\{-\left(-\frac{a-1}{a}\right)\right\}$ is
   - a $\frac{4}{5}$
   - b $-\frac{4}{5}$
   - c $-\frac{1}{\frac{1}{4}}$
   - d $-\frac{1}{4}$

9. The property of multiplication of rational numbers illustrated by the following statement is
   $$-\frac{5}{2} \times \frac{3}{4} + \frac{-5}{2} \times \frac{-6}{7} = \frac{-5}{2} \times \left(\frac{3}{4} - \frac{6}{7}\right)$$
   - a associativity
   - b distributivity
   - c commutativity
   - d None of these

10. If the fraction $4 + \cfrac{1}{m + \cfrac{1}{n}}$ is equivalent to the fraction $\frac{56}{12}$. Then, the value of $m + n$, where m and n are integers, is
    - a 2
    - b 3
    - c 5
    - d 8

11. If the numbers A, B, C, D, E, F, G and H are shown on the number line, then the value of the expression $(C + E) - (A + B) \div (G - H)$ is

A	B	C	D	E	F		G	H
$-\dfrac{9}{7}$	$-\dfrac{8}{7}$	$\dfrac{0}{5}$	$\dfrac{5}{7}$	$\dfrac{9}{11}$	$\dfrac{10}{11}$		$\dfrac{14}{6}$	$\dfrac{15}{6}$

  a $\dfrac{105}{77}$ b $\dfrac{77}{1059}$

  c $-\dfrac{1059}{77}$ d $-\dfrac{105}{77}$

12. Match the following:

List I		List II
A.	Additive inverse of $\dfrac{2}{3}$ is	i. x
B.	Multiplicative inverse of $\dfrac{2}{3}$ is	ii. $-x$
C.	If $y = \dfrac{1}{x}$, then $-\dfrac{1}{y}$ is	iii. $\dfrac{3}{2}$
D.	Reciprocal of x^{-1} is	iv. $-\dfrac{2}{3}$

Codes

	A	B	C	D
a	(i)	(ii)	(iii)	(iv)
b	(iv)	(iii)	(ii)	(i)
c	(iv)	(ii)	(iii)	(i)
d	(ii)	(iv)	(i)	(iii)

13. If the sum and product of two numbers are 12 and 35, respectively. Then, the sum of their reciprocals is

  a $\dfrac{7}{5}$

  b $\dfrac{12}{35}$

  c $-\dfrac{10}{14}$

  d None of the above

14. Find the odd one out from the given figures.

$\dfrac{2}{3} \times \dfrac{4}{5}$ $\dfrac{3}{5} \times \dfrac{-8}{9}$ $-\left(\dfrac{2}{5} \div \dfrac{4}{3}\right)$ $\dfrac{3}{6} \times \dfrac{1}{4}$

$\dfrac{2}{3} \times \left(\dfrac{4}{5} + \dfrac{5}{6}\right)$ $\dfrac{3}{5} \times \left(\dfrac{6}{7} - \dfrac{8}{9}\right)$ $\dfrac{2}{5} \div \left(\dfrac{5}{2} + \dfrac{4}{3}\right)$ $\dfrac{3}{6} \times \left(\dfrac{5}{7} + \dfrac{1}{4}\right)$

$\dfrac{2}{3} \times \dfrac{5}{6}$ $\dfrac{3}{5} \times \dfrac{6}{7}$ $\dfrac{2}{5} \div \dfrac{5}{2}$ $\dfrac{3}{6} \times \dfrac{5}{7}$

    A   B   C   D

  a A and C

  b Only C

  c A and B

  d C and D

15. **Assertion** (A) $a - (b - c) = (a - b) - c$

  Reason (R) Rational numbers are not associative under subtraction.

  Which of the following is true?

  a Both (A) and (R) are true and (R) is correct explanation of (A)

  b Both (A) and (R) are false and (R) is not correct explanation of (A)

  c (A) is true and (R) is false

  d (A) is false and (R) is true

16. State 'T' for true or 'F' for false.

  I. If $\dfrac{p}{q}$ is a rational number, then $p \neq 0$.

  II. If $\dfrac{b}{a}$ is multiplicative inverse of $\dfrac{a}{b}$, then $a \neq 0$.

  III. For any rational number x, $x + (-1) = -x$.

  IV. $\dfrac{x + y}{2}$ is a rational number which lies between x and y.

  V. The rational numbers $\dfrac{1}{2}$ and $-\dfrac{3}{6}$ are on the opposite sides of '0' on the number line.

Codes

	I	II	III	IV	V			I	II	III	IV	V
a	F	T	F	T	T		b	T	F	T	F	F
c	F	F	F	F	F		d	T	T	T	T	T

17. Fill in the blanks with the help of options, given in the box.

> (i) x^4,   (ii) $-\dfrac{7}{5}$,   (iii) $\dfrac{8}{3}$,   (iv) $-\dfrac{3}{2}$,   (v) 1,
>
> (vi) $x(x^2 + 1)$,   (vii) -1,   (viii) $\dfrac{3}{2}$,   (ix) $\dfrac{6}{3}$,   (x) $-\dfrac{5}{7}$,
>
> (xi) $\dfrac{9}{13}$,   (xii) 0

  I. $-(-x) \div x^{-1} \times x + x = $ ___ .

  II. $\left(\dfrac{3}{2} - \dfrac{2}{3}\right) - (-\Box) = -\dfrac{1}{6}$.

  III. If $m * n = \dfrac{m}{n} - \dfrac{n}{m}$, then $9 * 18 = $ ___ .

  IV. $(x + y) \div (x - y)$ for $x = \dfrac{1}{4}$, $y = \dfrac{3}{2}$ is ___ .

Codes

	I	II	III	IV
a	(i)	(ii)	(iii)	(v)
b	(vi)	(vii)	(iv)	(ii)
c	(vi)	(vii)	(viii)	(x)
d	(xi)	(xii)	(i)	(iii)

18. If the number $3254p06q$ is exactly divisible by 3 and 5, then the maximum value of $p+q$ is

    a 12   **b** 13
    c 14   **d** 15

19. If 16 shirts of equal size can be made out of 24 m cloth. The length of cloth needed for making 12 such shirts is

    a 15 m   **b** 18 m
    c 24 m   **d** 12 m

20. $\dfrac{2}{5}$th of the total number of students of a school come by car, while $\dfrac{1}{4}$th of rest of the students come to school by bus and the remaining 180 students come by walking. The total number of students is

    a 500   **b** 450
    c 400   **d** 300

21. If difference of $\dfrac{3}{5}$ and $\dfrac{2}{7}$ of a number is 44. Then, the sum of digits of that number is

    a 50   **b** 5
    c 14   **d** 4

22. Raju earns ₹ 12000 per month, he spends $\dfrac{1}{4}$ of his income on food, $\dfrac{3}{10}$ of remaining money on house rent and $\dfrac{5}{21}$ of remaining money on the education of his children. The money saved is

    a ₹ 4500   **b** ₹ 4800
    c ₹ 5000   **d** ₹ 1200

23. The following table:

Items	Cost
A. Hot dog	i. 5 for ₹ 60
B. Pastry	ii. 4 for ₹ 20
C. Roll	iii. 3 for ₹ 60

Raju bought 3 hot dogs, 2 pastries and 4 rolls. If he has total ₹ 200 in his pocket, then money left to the total money is represented in the form of $\left(\dfrac{p}{q}\right)$ i.e. rational number is

    a $\dfrac{37}{50}$ **b** $\dfrac{74}{200}$
    c $\dfrac{126}{200}$ **d** None of these

24. Three students gave an improvement test. Ajay scored $\dfrac{30}{60}$ in his first test and $\dfrac{35}{60}$ in improvement test. Sonu scored $\dfrac{42}{70}$ in his first test and $\dfrac{50}{60}$ in improvement test. Manish scored $\dfrac{50}{60}$ in his first test and $\dfrac{42}{50}$ in improvement test. Which student improved the most?

    a Ajay
    b Sonu
    c Manish
    d Ajay and Manish improved by same per cent.

25. One recipe requires $\dfrac{2}{5}$ cup of sugar. Another recipe for the same dish requires 5 tablespoons of sugar. If 1 tablespoon is equivalent to $\dfrac{1}{15}$ cup, then the more amount of sugar needed by the first recipe is

    a 1 tablespoon
    b 15 tablespoons
    c $\dfrac{1}{5}$ cup
    d 5 tablespoons

26. Mohan and Sohan each receives an annual allowance. The table shows the fraction of their allowance they used as follows:

	Fraction of allowance	Mohan	Sohan
A.	Saving account	$\dfrac{1}{2}$	$\dfrac{1}{3}$
B.	Spend at mall	...	$\dfrac{3}{5}$
C.	Left over	₹ 84	₹ 84

If total allowance is ₹1260 to each of them, then what will come in place of ...?

    a $\dfrac{7}{15}$ **b** $\dfrac{13}{30}$
    c $\dfrac{14}{30}$ **d** $\dfrac{9}{15}$

2 Exponent and Power

1. The value of given expression
$$(a^m \cdot a^n) \div (a^m / a^n)$$
is equal to, if $a = 2$ and $m, n \in$ integers.

   a 2^{2m+2n} b 2^{2n}

   c 2^{2m} d None of these

2. For a non-zero integer x, $(x^4)^{-3}$ is equal to

   a x^{12} b x^{-12} c x^{64} d x^{-64}

3. If $\dfrac{(-2)^x \times (-2)^7}{3 \times 4^6} = \dfrac{1}{12}$, then the value of x is

   a 3   b –3   c 2   d –4

4. The value of $-(-2)^3 - (-3)^2 + (-3)^4$ is equal to

   a 80   b 64

   c -82 d None of these

5. The value of $[1^{-2} + 2^{-2} + 3^{-2}] \times 6^2$ is equal to

   a 50   b 49   c 1/49   d 37

6. If $\dfrac{5^m \times 5^3 \times 5^{-2}}{5^{-3} \times 5^{-2}} = 5^{12}$, then the value of m is

   a 4   b 5   c 6   d 3

7. If $2^x + 2^x + 2^x = 192$, then the value of x is

   a 5   b 6   c 9   d 3

8. The value of m for which $\dfrac{(16)^{2m+1} \cdot (64)^5}{(256)^2 \cdot 4} = (256)^{3m}$, is

   a 1   b 0   c 4   d 5

9. What will come in the places of x and y respectively?

$$\boxed{(36)^{1/2}} - \boxed{\times (3)^2} - \boxed{\div (27)^{1/3}} - \boxed{= 3^x \times 2^y}$$

10. If $10^m \times 10^n \times 10^p = 10^6$, then the average of m, n and p is

   a 0   b 1   c 3   d 2

11. The value of $A + B$ that satisfies the given expression
$$(6^{30} + 6^{-30})(6^{30} - 6^{-30}) = 3^A \cdot 8^B - 3^{-A} \cdot 8^{-B}$$
is

   a 30   b 40   c 60   d 80

12. The value of $\dfrac{2^{2004} - 2^{2003}}{2^{2004} + 2^{2003}}$ is equal to

   a 0   b 2^{-2006} c $\dfrac{1}{3}$ d $\dfrac{1}{2}$

13. Match the following:

List I		List II	
A. $\left(-\dfrac{3}{2}\right)^3 \times x = \left(\dfrac{4}{27}\right)^{-2} \Rightarrow x =$	i.	-32	
B. $\dfrac{6^n}{6^{-2}} = 6^3 \Rightarrow n =$	ii.	n	
C. $4^{n-1} = \dfrac{1}{4} \cdot 4^y \Rightarrow y =$	iii.	1	
D. $-(3)^3 - (-3)^2 + (-2)^2 =$	iv.	$\dfrac{(-3)^3}{2}$	

Codes

	A	B	C	D		A	B	C	D
a	(i)	(ii)	(iii)	(iv)	b	(iv)	(iii)	(ii)	(i)
c	(iii)	(iv)	(i)	(ii)	d	(iv)	(iii)	(i)	(ii)

14. **Assertion** (A) $\quad 2^5 \div 2^2 = 8$

   Reason (R) $\quad a^m \div a^n = a^{m-n}$, according to the exponent rule.

Which of the following is true?
  - a Both (A) and (R) are true and (R) is the correct explanation of (A)
  - b Both (A) and (R) are false and (R) is not the correct explanation of (A)
  - c (A) is true and (R) is false
  - d (A) is false and (R) is true

15. The value of the expression
$$\left(\frac{81}{16}\right)^{-3/4} \times \left[\left(\frac{25}{9}\right)^{-3/2} \div \left(\frac{5}{2}\right)^{-3}\right] \text{ is}$$
  - a $\dfrac{6}{25}$
  - b $\dfrac{12}{125}$
  - c 1
  - d $-\left(\dfrac{5}{2}\right)^{-3}$

16. If $\dfrac{9^n \times 3^2 \times (3^{-n/2})^{-2} - (27)^n}{3^{3m} \times 2^3} = \dfrac{1}{27}$, then the relationship between m and n is
  - a $m + n = 1$
  - b $m - n = 1$
  - c $m = 1 - n$
  - d $\dfrac{m}{n} = 1$

17. If $\dfrac{8^{x+1}}{2^{x-x}} = 64$, then the value of 3^{2x+1} is equal to
  - a 1
  - b 3
  - c 9
  - d 27

18. The value of $\sqrt{2\dfrac{1}{4}} \times \left(1\dfrac{1}{3}\right)^2 + 1 \div \sqrt[3]{3\dfrac{3}{8}}$ is
  - a $3\dfrac{1}{3}$
  - b $4\dfrac{1}{6}$
  - c $1\dfrac{1}{3}$
  - d $5\dfrac{1}{2}$

19. The simplified value of the expression
$$\dfrac{2\cdot 3^{n+1} + 7\cdot 3^{n-1}}{3^{n+2} - 2\left(\dfrac{1}{3}\right)^{1-n}} \text{ is}$$
  - a 1
  - b 3
  - c -1
  - d 0

20. If $4^x + 4^x + 4^x + 4^x + 4^x + 4^x + 4^x + 4^x = \dfrac{1}{512}$, then the value of $-\dfrac{3}{x}$ is
  - a 0.5
  - b -8
  - c -0.75
  - d -4.25

21. If $3^x \times \dfrac{10}{3} - 3^{x-1} = 81$, then the value of x is
  - a 2
  - b 1
  - c 3
  - d 0

22. The cells of a bacterium double itself every hour. How many cells will there be after 10 h, if initially it is one cell?
  - a 512
  - b 256
  - c 1024
  - d 20

23.

I $\xrightarrow{\times 2^{-3}}$ II $\xrightarrow{\times 12^{-1}}$ III $\xrightarrow{\times 3^{-2}}$ 1/6

What will come in the IInd circle, if we follow the given pattern and final circle has 1/6?
  - a 72
  - b 18
  - c 288
  - d 120

24. A machine is like that, it takes input and then do some operations on it and provide the output. First it is multiplied by 2^2 and then result is multiplied by 3^2. After getting result, it is again multiplied by 6^{-2}. The result is, then multiplied by $\left(\dfrac{2}{3}\right)^{-1}$ and finally the result is divided by $\left(\dfrac{4}{3}\right)^{-1}$ and the output found is a smallest perfect square number of two digits. The input is
  - a 48
  - b 32
  - c 8
  - d 128

25. State 'T' for true or 'F' for false.
  - I. For any non-zero integer a, $a^{-m} = \dfrac{1}{a^m}$.
  - II. $(-1)^0 = -1$
  - III. The standard form for 0.0000048 is 4.8×10^{-6}.
  - IV. The $\dfrac{p}{q}$ form of the solution of $(4^{-1} + 8^{-1}) \div \left(\dfrac{2}{3}\right)^{-1}$ is $\dfrac{1}{8}$.
  - V. The reciprocal of $\left(\dfrac{2}{3}\right)^4$ is $\left(\dfrac{3}{2}\right)^4$.

Codes

	I	II	III	IV	V			I	II	III	IV	V
a	T	T	T	T	F		b	F	F	T	F	F
c	T	F	T	F	T		d	F	F	T	T	T

26. Fill in the blanks with the help of options, given in the box.

> (i) $-\left(\dfrac{1}{2}\right)^5$, (ii) $\dfrac{1}{81}$, (iii) 3, (iv) different,
> (v) $\left(\dfrac{5}{8}\right)$, (vi) same, (vii) 1, (viii) 0

  - I. $(-2)^{-5}$ is same as ___ .
  - II. The value of 4^{-2} and $(-2)^4$ are ___ .
  - III. $\left(\dfrac{8}{5}\right)^{-3} \div \left(\dfrac{5}{8}\right)^2 = $ ___ .
  - IV. If $\left(\dfrac{5}{2}\right)^{-4} \times \left(\dfrac{5}{2}\right)^{13} = \left(\dfrac{5}{2}\right)^{3x}$, then $x = $ ___ .
  - V. $\left[\left\{\left(-\dfrac{1}{3}\right)^2\right\}^{-2}\right]^{-1} = $ ___ .

Codes

	I	II	III	IV	V
a	(i)	(iv)	(v)	(iii)	(ii)
b	(ii)	(iii)	(iv)	(v)	(vi)
c	(vii)	(viii)	(i)	(ii)	(iii)
d	(iv)	(v)	(vi)	(vii)	(iii)

3

Square and Square Root

1. Which of the following is not a perfect square?
   - a 36
   - b 196
   - c 181
   - d 169

2. In a perfect square number, the last digit is given. Which of the following cannot be the last digit?
   - a 1
   - b 0
   - c 5
   - d 7

3. Which of the following letters best represents the location of $x - y$, where $x = \sqrt{169}$ and $y = \sqrt{64}$?

$$A \ B \ C \ D \ E$$
$$0 \ 1 \ 2 \ 3 \ 4 \ 5 \ 6$$

   - a B
   - b A
   - c D
   - d E

4. The sum of successive odd numbers from 1 to 20 is
   - a 81
   - b 100
   - c 64
   - d 49

5. If m is the square of a natural number n, then n is
   - a the square of m
   - b greater than m
   - c equal to m
   - d equal to $\sqrt{m}$

6. The value of expression $\sqrt{248 + \sqrt{52 + \sqrt{144}}}$ is
   - a 14
   - b 12
   - c 16
   - d 13

7. It is given that $\sqrt{4761} = 69$, then the value of $\sqrt{4761} + \sqrt{47.61} + \sqrt{0.4761}$ is
   - a 77
   - b 75.59
   - c 76.59
   - d 70.59

8. The two other numbers forming a Pythagorean triplet, whose third number is 5, are
   - a (3, 4)
   - b (−3, −4)
   - c (6, 4)
   - d (3, 7)

9. If $\sqrt{2 + \sqrt{x}} = 3$, then the value of x is
   - a 1
   - b $\sqrt{7}$
   - c $\sqrt{49}$
   - d 49

10. The smallest square number which is exactly divisible by each of the numbers 6, 9 and 15, is
    - a 100
    - b 400
    - c 900
    - d 1024

11. If $\sqrt{1 + \dfrac{27}{169}} = \left(1 + \dfrac{x}{13}\right)$, then the value of x is
    - a 1
    - b 3
    - c 5
    - d 7

12. What least number should be added to the number 6800, so that the resultant number is a perfect square?
    - a 24
    - b 76
    - c 89
    - d 256

13. The greatest five-digit number, which is a perfect square, is
    - a 99746
    - b 99856
    - c 90456
    - d 99999

MATHEMATICS OLYMPIAD CLASS VIII

14. The square root of $\dfrac{1.69}{0.0036} \times \dfrac{1.44}{6.76} \times \dfrac{0.25}{1.21}$ is

    a 4.54   b 4.75   c 4.95   d 4.99

15. Match the following:

	List I		List II
A.	Smallest perfect square	i.	17
B.	Sum of first 8 odd numbers	ii.	64
C.	Area of square is 144 cm^2, its perimeter is	iii.	1
D.	The least number added to sum of squares of first 5 prime numbers to form a perfect square	iv.	48

Codes

	A	B	C	D
a	(i)	(ii)	(iii)	(iv)
b	(iii)	(ii)	(iv)	(i)
c	(iii)	(iv)	(ii)	(i)
d	(ii)	(iv)	(iii)	(i)

16. Assertion (A) $1+3+5+7+9+11=36$.

Reason (R)   Sum of first n consecutive odd numbers is n^2.

Which of the following is true?

    a Both (A) and (R) are true and (R) is correct explanation of (A)

    b Both (A) and (R) are true but (R) is not correct explanation of (A)

    c (A) is true and (R) is false

    d (A) is false and (R) is true

17. If $\sqrt{188 + \sqrt{53 + \sqrt{y}}} = 14$, then the value of y is

    a 121   b 11   c 1331   d 161

18. The value of $\sqrt{6\sqrt{6\sqrt{6\sqrt{6}}}}$ is

    a 6^4 b $6^{1/4}$ c 3^6 d $6^{15/16}$

19. A group of students in a class collects ₹ 9216. The amount contributed by each student is equivalent to the number of students in the class. Then, total number of students is

    a 43   b 53   c 96   d 66

20. If $a = \sqrt{2} + 1$ and $b = \sqrt{2} - 1$, then the value of expression $\dfrac{a^2 - ab + b^2}{a^2 + ab + b^2}$ is

    a $32 - 4\sqrt{2}$ b $32 + 4\sqrt{2}$

    c 0   d $\dfrac{5}{7}$

21. If three numbers are in the ratio $1 : 2 : 3$ and the sum of their squares is 224. Then, the difference between the squares of greatest and least numbers, is

    a 80   b 160

    c 128   d 240

22. A person borrowed some money from a friend and promised him to pay daily for 1 month. He will pay like ₹ 1 for first day, ₹ 3 for second day, ₹ 5 for third day and so on for 30 days. If he paid an interest of ₹ 150 included in the above amount, then the money borrowed by him is

    a ₹ 600   b ₹ 750

    c ₹ 900   d ₹ 1200

23. State 'T' for true or 'F' for false.

    I. The sum of two perfect squares is a perfect square.

    II. The sum of first n even numbers is n^2.

    III. When a square number ends in 6, the number whose square it is, will have either 4 or 7 in unit's place.

    IV. The general form of Pythagorean triplet is $m^2 - 1, m^2 + 1, 2m + 1$.

    V. The square of a prime number is a prime number.

Codes

	I	II	III	IV	V			I	II	III	IV	V
a	F	F	F	F	F		b	T	F	T	F	T
c	T	T	T	T	T		d	F	T	F	T	F

24. Fill in the blanks with the help of options, given in the box.

> (i) 169, (ii) 144, (iii) 200, (iv) 400, (v) $2n + 1$, (vi) 8, (vii) 16, (viii) 9, (ix) 15, (x) 1, (xi) 4

    I. $1+3+5+7+9+11+13+15+17+19+21+23$ is ___ (find without adding)

    II. The value of $101^2 - 99^2$ is ___

    III. There are ___ natural numbers between n^2 and $(n+1)^2$.

    IV. The sides of a right angled triangle, whose hypotenuse is 17 cm, are ___ and ___ .

Codes

	I	II	III	IV
a	(ii)	(iv)	(v)	(vi), (ix)
b	(i)	(ii)	(iii)	(iv), (v)
c	(vii)	(viii)	(ix)	(x), (xi)
d	(ii)	(iii)	(iv)	(v), (vi)

4

Cube and Cube Root

1. Which of the following numbers is a perfect cube?

    a 1331   b 1441

    c 3475   d 2285

2. The cube root of $(-125) \times (-3375)$ is

    a 65   b -75

    c -85 d 75

3. Out of the following given numbers, which one is Hardy-Ramanujan number?

    a 2406   b 1729

    c 13833   d None of these

4. Which of the following is a cube of negative number?

    a 1331   b -729

    c 3375   d -1724

5. The value of the expression $\sqrt[3]{27} + \sqrt[3]{0.008} + \sqrt[3]{0.064}$ is

    a 9.7   b 3.6

    c 6.3   d 4.8

6. $\dfrac{14}{15}$ is the cube root of which of the following numbers?

    a $\dfrac{-2744}{3375}$ b $\dfrac{32764}{4485}$

    c $\dfrac{2744}{3375}$ d $\dfrac{-3375}{2744}$

7. If $32 * K$ (where * means multiplication) gives a perfect cube, then the value of K is

    a 3   b 2   c 5   d 8

8. The value of the expression $\sqrt[3]{288} \times \sqrt[3]{432} \times \sqrt[3]{648}$ is

    a 432   b 565

    c 469   d 328

9. If x and y are negative integers such that $x^2 > y^2$, then relation between x^3 and y^3 is

    a $x^3 < y^3$

    b $x^3 > y^3$

    c $x^3 = y^3$

    d None of the above

10. By what smallest number should 243 be divided, so that the quotient be a perfect cube. Then, the cube root of the quotient is

    a 81   b 3

    c 9   d None of these

11. Which smallest number should be added to the multiple of 4, 9 and 12 to make it a perfect cube?

    a 28   b 36   c 9   d 89

12. Match the following:

	List I		List II
A.	$\sqrt[6]{\left(\dfrac{91125}{216}\right)^2}$	i.	3
B.	Smallest cubic number is	ii.	$\dfrac{8}{5}$
C.	If $\sqrt[3]{4\dfrac{12}{125}} = x$, then x is	iii.	1
D.	If $(27)^{1/3} = 3$, then $\sqrt[3]{27}$ is	iv.	$\dfrac{45}{6}$

Codes

	A	B	C	D
a	(i)	(ii)	(iii)	(iv)
b	(iv)	(iii)	(ii)	(i)
c	(iv)	(ii)	(iii)	(i)
d	(ii)	(iv)	(i)	(iii)

MATHEMATICS OLYMPIAD CLASS VIII

13. If $\sqrt[3]{3\left(\sqrt[3]{x}-\dfrac{1}{\sqrt[3]{x}}\right)}=2$, then the value of $\left(x-\dfrac{1}{x}\right)$ is

  a $\dfrac{728}{9}$ b $\dfrac{72}{27}$

  c $\dfrac{728}{27}$ d $\dfrac{3}{15}$

14. Three numbers are in the ratio $2:3:4$ to one another. The sum of their cubes is 33957. Then, the difference in the cubes of greatest and smallest numbers is

  a 20000   b 21200

  c 19208   d 22208

15. **Assertion** (A) 1729 is a Hardy-Ramanujan number.

Reason (R) Cube of 12^3 is 1728.

Which of the following is true?

  a Both (A) and (R) are true and (R) is correct explanation of (A)

  b Both (A) and (R) are true but (R) is not the correct explanation of (A)

  c (A) is true and (R) is false

  d (A) is false and (R) is true

16. If cube of a number x is four times of x. Then, value of x, where $x > 0$, is

  a 8   b 2

  c 4   d 3

17. If surface area of a cube is $150\ \text{cm}^2$. Then, the volume of the cube will be

  a $25\ \text{cm}^3$ b $75\ \text{cm}^3$

  c $125\ \text{cm}^3$ d $27\ \text{cm}^3$

18. Find the odd one out from the given options.

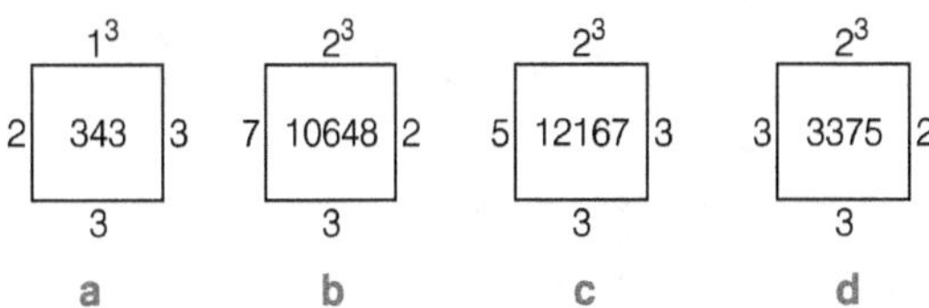

  a   b   c   d

19. In the given five-digit number $1A6B3$, B is the greatest single digit perfect cube and twice of it exceeds A by 7. Then, the sum of the above number and its cube root is

  a 18700

  b 11862

  c 19710

  d 25320

20. Which of the following is odd?

  a $2\times1+3^3=27+2=29$

  b $7\times2+2^3=14+8=22$

  c $5\times2+3^2=5\times11=55$

  d $3\times3+2^3=9+8=17$

21. State 'T' for true or 'F' for false.

  I. For any positive number n, $n^2 < n^3$.

  II. 1728 is a Hardy-Ramanujan number.

  III. Hardy-Ramanujan numbers can't be expressed as a sum of two cubes in two different ways.

  IV. As the square of negative number is positive, similarly the cube of negative number is also positive.

  V. For two natural numbers a and b, $a^3\times b^3=(a\times b)^3$.

Codes

	I	II	III	IV	V
a	T	F	F	F	T
b	T	F	T	F	T
c	F	T	F	T	F
d	F	F	T	T	T

22. Fill in the blanks with the help of options, given in the box.

> (i) $125\ \text{cm}^3$, (ii) $27\ \text{cm}^3$, (iii) 5, (iv) 8,
> (v) 6, (vi) 9, (vii) 3, (viii) 2, (ix) 4, (x) 7

  I. Volume of a cube, whose surface area is $54\ \text{cm}^2$, is ___ .

  II. The number of perfect cubes greater than 1 and less than 1000 is ___ .

  III. The least number by which 72 be divided to make it a perfect cube is ___ .

  IV. Unit digit of a cube of a number having 7 as unit the digit, will be ___ .

  V. If a^2 ends in 9, then a^3 ends in ___ or ___ .

Codes

	I	II	III	IV	V
a	(ii)	(iv)	(vi)	(vii)	(x),(vii)
b	(i)	(ii)	(iii)	(iv)	(v),(ix)
c	(vi)	(vii)	(viii)	(ix)	(x),(iii)
d	(x)	(v)	(iii)	(iv)	(i),(ix)

5

Algebraic Expressions

1. The degree of a constant polynomial is
   - a 1
   - b 2
   - c 0
   - d 3

2. Which of the following statements is true?
   - a $g(x) + g(y) = 2g(x)$
   - b $f(y) - f(x) = 0$
   - c $g(x) + 2g(x) = 3g(x)$
   - d All of the above

3. The difference of the degrees of the polynomials $5x^3 y^2 + 6xy^7 - x^6$ and $4x^5 - 4x^3 + 2$ is
   - a 2
   - b 3
   - c 1
   - d 0

4. Which of the following is a zero degree polynomial?
   - a $3x + 4y + 3$
   - b $(2x - 2)^2 + 4(x^2 - x - 1)$
   - c $0x^3 + 0y^3 + 0xy$
   - d Both (b) and (c)

5. $4x^3, 7x^2, 3xy, -7z$ are all examples of
   - a binomial
   - b trinomial
   - c monomial
   - d None of the above

6. Which of the following is a binomial?
   - a $(2 - 2x)^2 + 4x^3$
   - b $(5y - 4)^2 - y^2$
   - c $x - 2y + 1$
   - d None of these

7. Sum of $a - b + ab$, $b + c - bc$ and $c - a - ac$ is
   - a $2c + ab - ac - bc$
   - b $2c - ab - ac - bc$
   - c $2c + ab + ac + bc$
   - d $2c - ab + ac + bc$

8. What must be added to $x^3 + x^2 + x - 1$ to get $x^4 + 2x^2 - 3x + 7$?
   - a $x^4 - x^3 + x^2 - 4x + 8$
   - b $x^3 + x^2 - 4x + 8$
   - c $x^4 - x^3 + x^2 + 4x - 8$
   - d $x^4 - x^3 - x^2 + 4x - 8$

9. Product of $(x^2 + 3x + 5)$ and $(x^2 - 1)$ is
   - a $x^4 + 3x^3 - 4x^2 - 3x - 5$
   - b $x^4 + 3x^3 + 4x^2 - 3x - 5$
   - c $x^4 + 3x^3 + 4x^2 + 3x - 5$
   - d $x^4 + x^3 + x + 5$

10. The length of a rectangle is x m while its breadth is 5 less than twice its length. Write an expression to represent the perimeter of the rectangle.
    - a $6x - 10$
    - b $6x - 5$
    - c $3x + 5$
    - d $3x - 10$

MATHEMATICS OLYMPIAD CLASS VIII

11. Perimeter of a triangle is 20 m. Its length of sides are in the ratio $2:3:5$, then difference between its longest and smallest sides is

    a 4 m   b 6 m

    c 5 m   d 8 m

12. What is the quotient of the polynomial, if $y^3 - 6y^2 + 9y - 2$ is divided by $y - 2$?

    a $y^2 + 4y + 1$

    b $y^2 - 4y + 1$

    c $y^2 + 4y - 1$

    d $y^2 - 4y - 1$

13. The remainder when $5m^3 - 13m^2 + 15m + 7$ is divided by $4 - 3m + m^2$, is

    a $m + 1$ b $m - 1$

    c $2m + 1$ d $2m - 1$

14. Match the following:

	List I		List II
A.	$4x^2 - 20xy + 25y^2$ is	i.	$441x^2 + 169y^2 - 546xy$
B.	$(x + a)(x + b)$ is equal to, if $a = 2, b = 3$	ii.	$x^2 + 5x + 6$
C.	34×26 can be written in the form of	iii.	$(x + b)(x - b)$
D.	$(21x - 13y)(21x - 13y)$	iv.	$(2x - 5y)(2x - 5y)$

    Codes

	A	B	C	D
a	(i)	(ii)	(iii)	(iv)
b	(iv)	(ii)	(iii)	(i)
c	(iv)	(iii)	(ii)	(i)
d	(i)	(iii)	(ii)	(iv)

15.

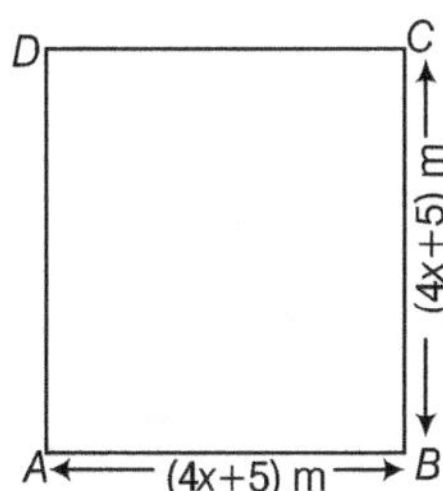

In the above figure, $ABCD$ is a square and its dimensions are given. If the area of the square is 625 m^2, then its perimeter will be

    a 25 m   b 100 m

    c 80 m   d 75 m

16. The area of rectangle is $x^2 + 7x + 12$. If its length is $(x + 3)$, then the breadth will be (when $x = 2$)

    a 6   b 8

    c 12   d 2

17. The value of $p^2 + q^2$, if it is given that $p + q = 12$ and $pq = 22$, is

    a 10   b 100

    c 144   d 12

18. The product of m and n, if difference between them is 16 and sum of their squares is 400, is

    a 72

    b 144

    c 36

    d None of the above

19. If $x - \dfrac{1}{x} = 7$, then the value of $x^2 + \dfrac{1}{x^2}$ is

    a 49   b 47

    c 51   d 53

20. Value of the given expression $\dfrac{6.25 \times 6.25 - 1.75 \times 1.75}{4.5}$ is

    a 5   b 8

    c 10   d 9

21. If the sum of a number and its reciprocal is 14. Then, the value of sum of the cubes of the number and its reciprocal is

    a 2072

    b 2027

    c 2772

    d 2702

22. The value of expression $\dfrac{2x^3 - 12x^2 + 16x}{(x - 2)(x - 4)}$ is

    a 2   b $\dfrac{x}{2}$

    c $2x$ d $2x^2$

23. **Assertion** (A) $6^2 + 8^2 = 10^2$

    Reason (R) $a^2 + b^2 = (a + b)^2$

    Which of the following is true?

    a Both (A) and (R) are true and (R) is the correct explanation of (A)

    b Both (A) and (R) are true and (R) is not the correct explanation of (A)

    c (A) is true and (R) is false

    d (A) is false and (R) is true

24. The value of the product $\left(2+\dfrac{4}{x}\right)\left(10-\dfrac{15}{x}+\dfrac{25}{x^2}\right)$

at $x=1$ is

   a 150

   b 120

   c 200

   d 240

25. The value of $(x+2)^3-(x-2)^3$ is

   a $12x^2+16$

   b 0

   c 1

   d $1-8x^3$

26. Fill in the blanks with the help of options, given in the box.

> (i) 36, (ii) 6, (iii) $x(a+b)$, (iv) $(a+b)$, (v) 1, (vi) 0, (vii) 81, (viii) 79, (ix) 4

  I. If $x^2+y^2=40$ and $x\times y=2$, then $x-y$ is ___ .

  II. $(x+a)(x+b)=x^2+$ ___ $+ab$.

  III. If $a=b=c$, then $a^2+b^2+c^2-ab-bc-ca$ is ___ .

  IV. If $x+\dfrac{1}{x}=9$, then $x^2+\dfrac{1}{x^2}=$ ___ .

  V. Coefficient of z^2 in the expression $x^2+4xz+4z^2$ is ___ .

Codes

	I	II	III	IV	V
a	(ii)	(iii)	(vi)	(viii)	(ix)
b	(i)	(ii)	(iii)	(iv)	(v)
c	(v)	(vii)	(viii)	(ix)	(vi)
d	(i)	(ii)	(ix)	(vi)	(iii)

27. State 'T' for true or 'F' for false.

  I. $a^2-b^2=(a-b)^2$.

  II. An identity is true for all values of its variables.

  III. On dividing $\dfrac{x}{4}$ by $\dfrac{4}{x}$, then the quotient is 16.

  IV. $(5x-63)\div 9=5x-7$.

  V. The value of p for $64^2-56^2=120\,p$, is 8.

Codes

	I	II	III	IV	V
a	F	T	F	F	T
b	T	T	T	T	F
c	T	F	T	F	T
d	F	T	F	T	T

28. The perimeter of a triangle is $8p^2-9p+9$ and two of its sides are $2p^2-3p+1$ and $5p^2-p+4$. Then, third side of the triangle is

   a $2p^2-6p+5$

   b p^2-5p+4

   c $3p^2-2p+1$

   d $4p^2+3p+6$

6

Factorisation of Algebraic Expressions

1. The factor of $6 - y - 2y^2$ is
   - a $y + 2$
   - b $y - 3$
   - c $-2y + 3$
   - d Both (a) and (c)

2. After factorising $x^3 - 27$, the factors can be written in the form of
   - a $(x - 3)(x^2 + 3x + 9)$
   - b $(x + 3)(x^2 + 3x + 9)$
   - c $(x - 3)(x^2 - 3x + 9)$
   - d $(x - 3)(x^2 + 3x - 9)$

3. After factorising $10x^2 + 21x + 9$, we see that the factors are in the form of $(2x + 3)(5x + 3)$. So, the factors of 1219 can be written as, (x is a natural number)
   - a 53×33
   - b 23×53
   - c 33×23
   - d None of these

4. It is given that $4x^2 - 12xy + 9y^2 = 0$. Then, the value of $\dfrac{2x}{3y}$ is
   - a $-1/2$
   - b 1
   - c $1/2$
   - d Can't say

5. If we factorise $xy - pq + qy - px$. The factors, thus obtained are
   - a $(y - p)(x + q)$
   - b $(y - p)(x - q)$
   - c $(y + p)(x + q)$
   - d $(y + p)(x - q)$

6. One of the factors of $x^4 - (x - z)^4$ is given by
   - a $2x + z$
   - b $x + 2z$
   - c $2x - z$
   - d $x - 2z$

7. Value of expression $\dfrac{58^2 - 42^2}{16}$ is
   - a 1
   - b 90
   - c 100
   - d 0

8. If $y^2 + 18y + 65 = ay^2 + 2by + 65$. Then, the value of $\dfrac{(a + b)}{(a - b)}$ is
   - a $\dfrac{19}{18}$
   - b $-\dfrac{5}{4}$
   - c $\dfrac{4}{5}$
   - d Can't say

9. If $(x^3y^3 + x^2y^3 - xy^4 + xy) \div xy$ and quotient is factorised, then factors of quotient are
   - a $(x + 1)$
   - b $(y - 1)$
   - c Can't factorise
   - d $x^2 - y^2$

10. Match the following:

List I		List II	
A.	One factor of $p^5 - 16p$ is	i.	3
B.	Real factor of $x^2 + 16$ is	ii.	Can't be calculated
C.	$p^3 - q^3 = (p - q) \times (...)$	iii.	$p - 2$
D.	If $x^2 + \dfrac{1}{x^2} = 7$, then $x + \dfrac{1}{x}$ is	iv.	$p^2 + pq + q^2$

Codes

	A	B	C	D
a	(i)	(ii)	(iii)	(iv)
b	(iii)	(ii)	(iv)	(i)
c	(iii)	(iv)	(i)	(ii)
d	(iii)	(iv)	(ii)	(i)

11. One of the factors of $x^2 + \dfrac{1}{x^2} + 2 - 2x - \dfrac{2}{x}$ is given by

  a $x - \dfrac{1}{x}$ **b** $x + \dfrac{1}{x} - 1$ **c** $x + \dfrac{1}{x} - 2$ **d** $x^2 + \dfrac{1}{x^2}$

12. In factorisation, we use various techniques to do so. One of the techniques is illustrated here.

Step I $x^2 - 13x + 42$

Step II $x^2 - 7x - 6x + 42$

Step III $x^2 - 13x + 42 + 13 - 13$

Step IV $x(x-7) - 6(x-7)$

Step V Factors are $(x-6)$ and $(x-7)$.

Which of the following steps shown above is wrong?

  a I   **b** II   **c** IV   **d** III

13. Which method is used in the factorisation shown below?

(i) $x^2 + 8x + 16$

(ii) $(x)^2 + (4)^2 + 2 \cdot x \cdot 4$

(iii) $(x+4)^2$; $(a+b)^2 = a^2 + b^2 + 2ab$

(iv) $(x+4)(x+4)$

  a Splitting middle term
  b Completing square
  c Algebraic identity
  d None of the above

14. A student is asked to factorise the expression $6x^2 - 30x + 36$ and after factorising, he found his answers are 6, $(x+3)$ and $(x+2)$. Another student while factorising same expression found that the first student has made a mistake and after correcting it, he gave the right answer. What were the correct factors?

  a $(x+3)(x-2)$ **b** $(x-3)(x+2)$
  c $(x-3)(x-2)$ **d** No error

15. If $(x^2 + 3x + 5)(x^2 - 3x + 5) = m^2 - n^2$, then m is

  a $x^2 - 3x$ **b** $3x$ **c** $x^2 + 5$ **d** $3x + 5$

16. Choose the odd one from the given algebraic expressions.

  (A) $x^2 - 4x + 4$ (B) $x^2 - 5x + 6$
  (C) $x^2 - 9x + 18$ (D) $3x^2 - 24x + 36$

  a A   **b** B   **c** C   **d** D

17. $\dfrac{0.87 \times 0.87 \times 0.87 + 0.13 \times 0.13 \times 0.13}{1.0}$

$= p \times (0.87)^2 + q(0.87 \times 0.13) + r(0.13)^2$

In the given expression, what will be the value of $(p - q - r)$?

  a 1   **b** 2   **c** 3   **d** −1

18. The figure shows, the dimensions of a wall having a window and a door at a room.

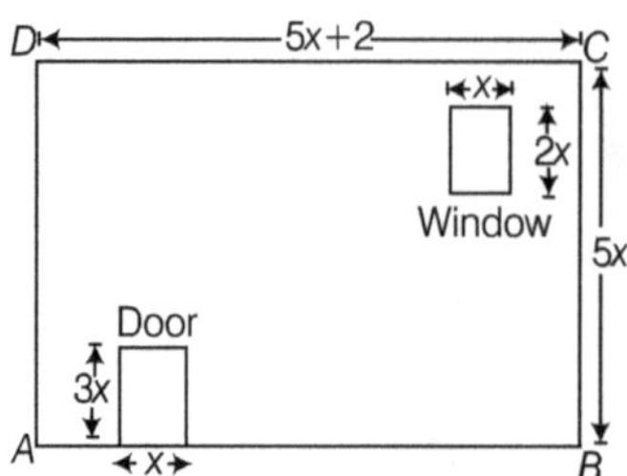

Area of wall to be painted at the rate ₹ 5 sq units. The cost charged is ₹ 50. Then, perimeter of wall is

  a 10 units   **b** 12 units
  c 14 units   **d** 7 units

19. Fill in the blanks with the help of options, given in the box.

> (i) $2x + 3$, (ii) $2x - 3$, (iii) $6x^2 + 8x$,
> (iv) $8x^2 + 6x$, (v) 140, (vi) 110, (vii) $12x - 12y$,
> (viii) $16x - 12y$, (ix) 23, (x) 22

  I. $8x^2 - 18x + 9 = (4x - 3) \times \underline{\quad}$.

  II. $64x^4 - 36x^2 = (8x^2 - 6x) \times \underline{\quad}$.

  III. If $x + \dfrac{1}{x} = 5$, then $x^3 + \dfrac{1}{x^3} = \underline{\quad}$.

  IV. Area of a square field is $16x^2 + 9y^2 - 24xy$. The perimeter of that field is $\underline{\quad}$.

  V. If $m + n = 45$ and $m^2 - n^2 = 45$, then $m = \underline{\quad}$.

Codes

	I	II	III	IV	V
a	(ii)	(iv)	(vi)	(viii)	(ix)
b	(i)	(ii)	(iii)	(iv)	(v)
c	(vi)	(vii)	(viii)	(ix)	(x)
d	(ii)	(iv)	(vi)	(viii)	(x)

20. State 'T' for true or 'F' for false.

  I. The factors of $x^2 - 6x + 9$ is $(x-3)(x-3)$.

  II. The difference of squares of two numbers is their sum multiplied by their difference.

  III. $x^2 - (a+b)x + ab = (x-a)(x+b)$

  IV. Regrouping is not a method of factorisation.

  V. The process of writing a given expression as the product of two or more factors is called factorisation.

Codes

	I	II	III	IV	V			I	II	III	IV	V
a	T	T	F	F	T		b	T	F	T	T	T
c	F	F	F	T	F		d	T	T	F	F	F

7

Linear Equation in One Variable

1. The highest power of a variable in linear equation in one variable is
   - a 1
   - b 2
   - c 3
   - d any number

2. The correct value of x in the equation $\dfrac{x-2}{x+3}=\dfrac{3}{8}$ is
   - a 3
   - b 4
   - c 5
   - d 10

3. The linear form of the equation $\dfrac{7x+5}{8x+6}=\dfrac{2}{3}$ is given by
   - a $3(7x+5)-2(8x+6)=0$
   - b $5x=3$
   - c $3(7x+6)-2(8x+5)=0$
   - d $5x-3=0$

4. $x=-2$ is the solution of the equation
   - a $6x-3=3x-5$
   - b $x-3=x+4$
   - c $5x-3=3x-7$
   - d $7x-6=6x-5$

5. For what value of a, the expression $\dfrac{a-8}{5}$ is equal to $\dfrac{a-6}{3}$?
   - a 7
   - b 3
   - c 12
   - d 5

6. The solution of which of the following equations is neither an odd nor an even?
   - a $3y+2=4y+2$
   - b $4z-18=6$
   - c $3x+7=5x+3$
   - d $5y-8=y+4$

7. Which of the following is a linear expression?
   - a x^2+3
   - b $z+z^2$
   - c 7
   - d $1+x$

8. Which of the following is a linear equation in one variable?
   - a $(2x-2)^2=4x^2+4x-4$
   - b $(3x-4)^2=3x-3x^2+3$
   - c $x^2=2x-2$
   - d All of the above

9. Raju's present age is five years more than thrice of Shyam. If Shyam's age three years hence will be x years, then what is Raju's present age, if the sum of their present ages is 25 yr?
   - a 5 yr
   - b 15 yr
   - c 20 yr
   - d 32 yr

10. If sum of four consecutive multiples of 9 is 270. Then, x and the average of the numbers are respectively
    - a 50 and 54.5
    - b 54 and 67.5
    - c 50 and 70.5
    - d 54 and 810

11. If $\left(\dfrac{2}{3}\right)$rd of a number is multiplied by $\dfrac{3}{4}$, the resulting number is 6. Then, the number is

    a 9   b 12

    c 36   d 54

12. The value of x in the given linear equation in one variable is

$$\frac{x}{3} - \frac{1}{4}\left(x - \frac{1}{2}\right) = \frac{1}{8}(x+1) + \frac{1}{12}$$

    a 2   b −2

    c 12   d 16

13. Match the following:

	List I	List II
A.	If $8x - 5 - 3x = 6x - 4x + 4$, then x is	i. −1
B.	Number of solution for a linear equation in one variable is	ii. 3
C.	If x is three times the smallest prime number and also five times less than the smallest two-digit prime number, then x is	iii. 1
D.	If $\dfrac{5}{y} + 7 = \dfrac{2}{y} + 4$, then y is	iv. 6

Codes

	A	B	C	D
a	(i)	(ii)	(iii)	(iv)
b	(ii)	(iii)	(iv)	(i)
c	(ii)	(iv)	(iii)	(i)
d	(iii)	(ii)	(i)	(iv)

14. The solution of the linear equation $3x + 2y = 75$, if y is 5 more than x, is

    a $x = 13$ b $y = 8$

    c $x = 18$ d $y = 15$

15. The age of a man is same as his wife's age with the digits reversed. The sum of their ages is 99 yr and the man is 9 yr older than his wife. The age of man is

    a 54 yr

    b 45 yr

    c 63 yr

    d 36 yr

16. The length of a rectangle is 6 m less than three times its breadth, if perimeter of the rectangle is 148 m. Another rectangle having perimeter twice of the given rectangle and having the same relation between the dimensions of second rectangle as that of the first rectangle. Then, the length and breadth of second rectangle will be

    a 54 m and 20 m

    b 20 m and 54 m

    c 109.5 m and 38.5 m

    d None of the above

17. The denominator of a rational number is greater than its numerator by 2. If 2 is added to the denominator and 2 is subtracted from numerator, the new number becomes $\dfrac{1}{3}$. Then, ratio of the numerator and denominator of the given number (original number) is

    a $\dfrac{2}{3}$ b $\dfrac{5}{7}$

    c $\dfrac{7}{5}$ d $\dfrac{3}{2}$

18. Two years ago, Mohan was three times as old as his son and two years hence, twice his age will be equal to five times that of his son. Then, the present age of Mohan is

    a 14 yr   b 38 yr

    c 32 yr   d 34 yr

19. Choose the odd one from the given series.

    a $\dfrac{3x - 5}{6} = \dfrac{x}{3}$ b $\dfrac{z}{3} - \dfrac{1}{3} = \dfrac{4}{3}$

    c $6y + 7 = 3y + 22$ d $\dfrac{7y - 1}{4} = \dfrac{10}{3}$

20. If the number whose one-fifth part when increased by 30, is equal to its one-fourth part decreased by 30. Then, the number is

    a 120

    b 180

    c 1200

    d 1800

21. The perimeter of a rectangle is 240 cm. If its length is increased by 10% and its breadth is decreased by 20%, we get the same perimeter. Then, the length and breadth of the rectangle are

    a 80 cm and 40 cm

    b 40 cm and 80 cm

    c 40 cm and 60 cm

    d None of the above

22. Which of the following equations having $x = 12$, as its solution?

    a $\dfrac{x}{3} - \dfrac{x}{2} = 8$ b $\dfrac{x}{3} - \dfrac{x}{4} = 16$

    c $\dfrac{x}{2} + \dfrac{x}{3} - \dfrac{x}{4} = 7$ d $\dfrac{2x}{3} = \dfrac{8}{12} - \dfrac{0.25}{3}$

MATHEMATICS OLYMPIAD CLASS VIII

23. State 'T' for true or 'F' for false.

 I. $x^2 + 2$ is a linear equation in one variable.

 II. The terms linear equation and linear expression are same.

 III. If x is an odd number, then the next even number is $(2x + 1)$.

 IV. If both sides of an equation is to be divided by the same number (non-zero), then there is a change in equality.

 V. 1 is the solution of $\dfrac{x}{2} - \dfrac{4}{5} + \dfrac{x}{5} + \dfrac{3x}{10} = \dfrac{1}{5}$.

Codes

	I	II	III	IV	V
a	T	F	T	F	T
b	T	T	T	T	T
c	F	F	F	F	T
d	F	T	F	F	F

24. Fill in the blanks with the help of options, given in the box.

> (i) lowest, (ii) variable, (iii) −19, (iv) 10, (v) 4, (vi) 5, (vii) 20, (viii) 22, (ix) solution, (x) highest

 I. In a linear equation, the ___ power of the variable appearing in the equation is one.

 II. On subtracting 9 from product of p and 5, the result is found 11. Then, the value of p is ___ .

 III. Suman and Ojus have organised a party. They bought some pastries and some paneer tikkas whose total cost is ₹ 300. If both the items are equal in number and cost of pastries item is $\dfrac{2}{3}$ rd of paneer tikkas. Then, the number of paneer tikkas, if cost of it is ₹ 9 per piece, is ___ .

 IV. The value of the variable which, when substituted for the variable in an equation makes LHS = RHS, is called ___ of the given equation.

 V. If $\dfrac{2}{5x} - \dfrac{5}{3x} = \dfrac{1}{15}$, then $x =$ ___ .

Codes

	I	II	III	IV	V
a	(x)	(v)	(vii)	(ix)	(iii)
b	(i)	(ii)	(iii)	(iv)	(v)
c	(vi)	(vii)	(viii)	(ix)	(x)
d	(ii)	(iv)	(vi)	(viii)	(x)

8

Profit, Loss and Discount

1. Discount on any item is calculated on which of the following prices?
   - a Cost price
   - b Selling price
   - c Marked price
   - d Profit

2. A shopkeeper sold an article at 20% profit, that means he has got 20% extra on which of the price?
   - a Cost price
   - b Selling price
   - c Marked price
   - d None of the above

3. The selling price of goods which cost ₹ 10 and sold at a gain of 10%, is
   - a ₹ 12
   - b ₹ 11
   - c ₹ 9
   - d ₹ 11.10

4. A man sells a mare for ₹ 1085 making a profit of $8\dfrac{1}{2}\%$. The cost price of mare is
   - a ₹ 982
   - b ₹ 999.50
   - c ₹ 927.75
   - d ₹ 1000

5. Equivalent discount of 20%, 10% and 10% is
   - a 40%
   - b 35%
   - c 35.2%
   - d 65%

6. A man buys 5 oranges in ₹ 6 and sells 6 oranges in ₹ 5. In this transaction, he experiences loss. To gain 20% profit, what should be the selling rate of oranges?
   - a ₹ 2 per orange
   - b ₹ 1 per orange
   - c ₹ 1.44 per orange
   - d None of the above

7. The marked price of an article is ₹ 500. The shopkeeper gives a discount of 5% and still makes a profit of 25%. Then, how much did the article cost?
   - a ₹ 400
   - b ₹ 350
   - c ₹ 380
   - d ₹ 450

8. Lemons are bought ₹ 48 per dozen and sold at the rate of ₹ 40 per 10 lemons. During this business, what is percentage profit or loss occurred?
   - a 10% profit
   - b 10% loss
   - c No profit or loss
   - d None of the above

9. The marked price of a pen is increased by 20% and then a discount of 20% is allowed. If MRP is not increased and discount of 20% is offered. Then, by how much per cent is the selling price changed?
   - a 25%
   - b 20%
   - c −20%
   - d −10%

10. Match the following:

	List I		List II
A.	If CP = 150, loss per cent = 20%, then SP =	i.	Profit
B.	If SP = 250, profit per cent = 25%, then CP =	ii.	₹ 120
C.	If profit = 10% and loss = 10%, then (successive) resultant will be	iii.	₹ 200
D.	If SP > CP, then ... occurs.	iv.	1% loss

Codes

	A	B	C	D
a	(i)	(ii)	(iii)	(iv)
b	(ii)	(iii)	(iv)	(i)
c	(ii)	(iv)	(iii)	(i)
d	(ii)	(i)	(iii)	(iv)

11. A sells a bicycle to B at a profit of 30% and B sells it to C at a loss of 20%. If C pays ₹ 520 for it. Then, at what price did A buy?

   a ₹ 450

   b ₹ 500

   c ₹ 600

   d ₹ 550

12. Two stores A and B charge ₹ 750 for a video game. This week, there is sale offer on both the stores. The video game available at store B is of ₹ 600 and 25% off at store A. At which store, the video game is less expensive?

   a A

   b B

   c Same at A and B

   d None of the above

13. A dealer sold a radio at a loss of 2.5%. Had he sold it for ₹ 100 more, he would have gained 7.5%. For what value should he sell it in order to gain $12\frac{1}{2}\%$?

   a ₹ 1000   b ₹ 1125

   c ₹ 1250   d ₹ 1500

14. Divya purchased 20 dozens notebooks at ₹ 48 per dozen. She sold 8 dozens at 10% profit and remaining at 20% profit. What is his total profit percentage in this transaction?

   a 16%   b 30%

   c 15%   d 25%

15. Choose odd one from the given figures.

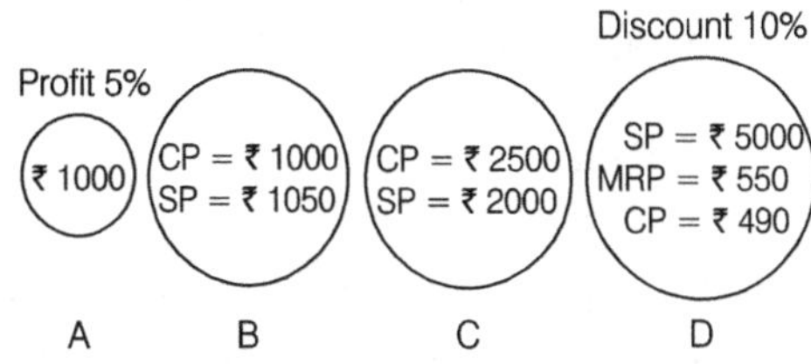

   a A

   b B

   c C

   d D

16. A, B and C marked an article at ₹ 5000 each. A sold it after giving successive discounts of 20% and 40%. B sold it after giving a 60% discount. C sold it after giving two successive discounts of 30% each. The maximum selling price (in ₹) is

   a 2400   b 2450

   c 2000   d 1600

17. State 'T' for true or 'F' for false.

  I. If selling price is less than cost price, then profit occurs.

  II. Discount per cent is calculated on SP.

  III. On selling a fan for ₹ 810, the gain is 8%. Then, CP of fan is ₹ 750.

  IV. The marked price is always fixed more than selling price.

  V. CP = MRP − Discount

Codes

	I	II	III	IV	V			I	II	III	IV	V
a	F	F	T	T	F		b	T	T	T	T	F
c	F	T	T	T	F		d	T	T	T	F	T

18. Fill in the blanks with the help of options, given in the box.

> (i) 800, (ii) 4.5, (iii) 195, (iv) discount, (v) 2.5, (vi) $11\frac{1}{9}\%$, (vii) 1000, (viii) 199.5, (ix) Sales tax, (x) 10%

  I. ___ is charged on the sale of an item by the government and is added to the bill amount.

  II. In the first year, on an investment of ₹ 60000, the loss is 5% and in the second year, the gain is 10%. The net result after 2 yr is ___ % gain.

  III. A vendor losses the selling price of 4 oranges on selling 36 oranges. His loss % is ___ .

  IV. The marked price of an article when it is sold for ₹ 880 after a discount of 12%, is ___ .

  V. 5% sales tax is charged on an article marked ₹ 200 after allowing a discount of 5%, then amount payable is ___ .

Codes

	I	II	III	IV	V
a	(ix)	(ii)	(vi)	(vii)	(viii)
b	(i)	(ii)	(iii)	(iv)	(v)
c	(vi)	(vii)	(viiii)	(ix)	(x)
d	(ii)	(iv)	(vi)	(ix)	(i)

9

Simple and Compound Interest

1. Simple interest and compound interest compounded yearly on a principal amount for 1 yr, has a relation
   - a SI = CI
   - b SI > CI
   - c CI > SI
   - d None of the above

2. A certain sum doubles in two years at r% rate of simple interest per annum or at R% rate of compound interest per annum compounded annually. We have,
   - a $r < R$
   - b $r = R$
   - c $r > R$
   - d Can't say

3. A sum is taken for three years at 10% per annum. If interest is compounded after every three months, then the number of times for which interest is changed in three years, is
   - a 8
   - b 12
   - c 6
   - d 9

4. If a sum of money is borrowed at 5% compound interest and paid back in two annual instalments of ₹ 882 each. Then, the sum borrowed was
   - a ₹ 1600
   - b ₹ 1640
   - c ₹ 1680
   - d ₹ 1700

5. If a sum of money becomes $\dfrac{216}{125}$ times itself in 3 yr, interest compounded annually, then rate of interest is
   - a 10%
   - b 20%
   - c 30%
   - d 40%

6. Anita borrowed a sum of money from Raju at the rate of 5% per annum compound interest for two years. She returned ₹ 5000 on the end of first year. At the end of second year, she returned ₹ 3820. The principal borrowed was
   - a ₹ 8000
   - b ₹ 8500
   - c ₹ 9000
   - d ₹ 7500

7. Suppose for principal P, rate R% and time T, the simple interest is S and compound interest is C. Consider the possibilities
   (i) $C - S > 0$ (ii) $C = S$ (iii) $C - S < 0$
   - a Only (i) is correct.
   - b Either (i) or (ii) is correct.
   - c Either (ii) or (iii) is correct.
   - d Only (iii) is correct.

8. Mehak and Monisha borrowed ₹ 62500 and ₹ 60000 respectively for a period of 2 yr. Mehak paid simple interest at the rate of 4% per annum, while Monisha paid compound interest at the same rate compounded annually. Who paid more interest and by how much?
   - a Mehak paid more by ₹ 104
   - b Monisha paid more by ₹ 104
   - c Both paid equal
   - d None of the above

9. If m, n and p are the three sums of money such that n is the simple interest on m and p is the simple interest on n for the same time and at the same rate of interest. The relation among m, n and p is given by
   - a $n^2 = mp$
   - b $m^2 = np$
   - c $p^2 = nm$
   - d $p = mn$

10. If the difference between the simple interest and compound interest on a certain sum of money lent (in each case) for two years is ₹ 1800. If the simple interest for two years is ₹ 28800, then sum in each case is

    a ₹ 105200   **b** ₹ 125200

    c ₹ 115200   **d** ₹ 135200

11. A sum of ₹ 1550 was lent partly at 5% and partly at 8% per annum simple interest. The total amount (interest) received after three years is ₹ 300. The ratio of the money lent on 5% and that of 8% are

    a 5 : 8   **b** 8 : 5

    c 16 : 15   **d** 31 : 6

12. Match the following:

	List I		List II
A.	$SI = CI$ for $T =$	i.	4
B.	$A = P\left(1 + \dfrac{r}{100}\right)^?$	ii.	n
C.	$P = 500, r = 10\%, SI = 40, T =$	iii.	1 yr
D.	$T = 2$ yr, if CI calculated half yearly, then $n =$	iv.	$\dfrac{4}{5}$ yr

Codes

	A	B	C	D
a	(i)	(ii)	(iii)	(iv)
b	(iii)	(ii)	(iv)	(i)
c	(iii)	(i)	(ii)	(iv)
d	(ii)	(i)	(iv)	(iii)

13. The CI on a certain sum for two years is ₹ 410 and SI on the same sum is ₹ 400. The rate of interest per annum is

    a 10%   **b** 8%   **c** 5%   **d** 4%

14. Rahul borrowed some amount at the rate of 6% per annum for first two years, at the rate of 9% per annum for next three years and at the rate of 14% for the period beyond five years at simple interest. If he pays a total interest of ₹ 11400 at the end of nine years, then how much amount did he borrow?

    a ₹ 12000   **b** ₹ 13000

    c ₹ 11000   **d** ₹ 14000

15. Karishma invested a certain amount in a market policy and found that it becomes ₹ 9680 in two years and become ₹ 10648 in three years compounded annually. The rate of interest given on the sum of money by the policy is

    a 10%   **b** 5%

    c 8%   **d** 12%

16. The population of a village is 8000. It increases by 10% during first year and by 20% during second year. Due to malaria in third year, the population decreases by 20%. The population of village after three years is

    a 8500   **b** 8448   **c** 8400   **d** 8800

17. State 'T' for true or 'F' for false.

    I. The CI and SI on the same principal for same time period and at same rate of interest are also equal. $(t > 1)$

    II. Simple interest is calculated by using the formula, $SI = P\left(1 + \dfrac{r}{100}\right)^n$.

    III. Compound interest is the interest calculated on previous year's amount.

    IV. The population of a city whose growth rate is known, is calculated by using the compound interest formula.

    V. If a sum of ₹ 1000 becomes 1331 after three years, then rate of interest is 10% per annum.

Codes

	I	II	III	IV	V			I	II	III	IV	V
a	F	F	T	T	T		b	F	T	F	T	T
c	T	F	T	F	T		d	T	T	T	T	F

18. Fill in the blanks with the help of options, given in the box.

> (i) 40%, (ii) 2.5%, (iii) 4, (iv) ≥, (v) 2, (vi) >,
> (vii) ₹ 1000, (viii) ₹ 10000, (ix) 1655.06,
> (x) 12155.06

    I. CI = ___, if $P = 10500$, $R = 5\%$ per annum and $T = 3$ yr.

    II. Rate = 10% per annum, when compounded quarterly for 1 yr by the formula, $A = P\left(1 + \dfrac{r}{100}\right)^n$, $r = $ ___ .

    III. If difference in CI and SI for a period of three years at the rate of 10% per annum on a fixed sum is 31, then $P = $ ___ .

    IV. Amount after n years, compounded quarterly is $P\left(1 + \dfrac{R}{\underline{\quad} \times 100}\right)^n$.

    V. CI is always ___ than SI for time period more than 1 yr.

Codes

	I	II	III	IV	V
a	(ix)	(ii)	(vii)	(iii)	(vi)
b	(i)	(ii)	(iii)	(iv)	(v)
c	(vi)	(vii)	(viii)	(ix)	(x)
d	(x)	(vii)	(ii)	(iv)	(i)

Direct and Inverse Proportion

1. In case of direct variation, between x and y, which of the following is true?

   a $xy = K$
   b $\dfrac{x}{y} = K$
   c $\dfrac{K}{y} = x$
   d $\dfrac{x}{K} = y$

2. If x and y are directly proportional and when $x = 10$, $y = 25$, then which of the following is a possible pair of corresponding values of x and y?

   a 1 and 3
   b 2 and 5
   c 15 and 60
   d 4 and 8

3. Both u and v vary inversely with each other, when u is 15, v is 5. Then, which of the following is not a possible pair of corresponding values?

   a 25 and 3
   b 10 and 7.5
   c 15 and 4
   d 30 and 2.5

4. A car needs 54 L of diesel for covering a distance of 297 km. The more diesel required to cover a distance of 550 km is

   a 100 L
   b 50 L
   c 46 L
   d 25 L

5. Complete the table given below.

Weight of rice (in kg)	3	2	—	4
Cost (in ₹)	105	—	210	140

   a 80, 6
   b 70, 8
   c 70, 6
   d 4, 135

6. The ratio of ages of a son and his mother five years ago was 2 : 5. After five years, the ratio will become 4 : 7. The present age of son is

   a 10 yr
   b 15 yr
   c 20 yr
   d 8 yr

7. Observe the following and choose the correct option.

x	6	12	18	24	15	9
y	4	8	12	16	10	6

   a $x \propto y$
   b $x \propto \dfrac{1}{y}$
   c $xy = K$
   d None of the above

8. In a camp, there are 100 persons and there is food available for 24 days for all of them. Due to some reasons, 20 persons come into the camp. How many days they will enjoy the food?

   a 10
   b 15
   c 20
   d 30

9. If a deposit of ₹ 5000 earns an interest of ₹ 1000 in 3 yr, then how much interest would a deposit of ₹ 30000 earn in 3 yr with the same rate of simple interest?

   a ₹ 3000
   b ₹ 5000
   c ₹ 6000
   d ₹ 10000

MATHEMATICS OLYMPIAD CLASS VIII

10. Match the following:

List I		List II
A. If $x \propto y$, then ___	i.	8
B. x and y are inversely proportionate, then ___	ii.	decreases
C. If $l = 5$, $m = 15$, then (if $l \propto m$) $m = 24$, $l =$ ___	iii.	$xy = $ constant
D. For $xy = K$, if x increases, then y ___	iv.	$x = Ky$

Codes

	A	B	C	D
a	(i)	(ii)	(iii)	(iv)
b	(iv)	(iii)	(i)	(ii)
c	(iv)	(i)	(iii)	(ii)
d	(ii)	(iv)	(iii)	(i)

11. A school has 8 periods in a day each of 30 min duration. What will be duration of each period, if school has decided to 10 periods a day and keeping the school hours same?

   a 30 min   b 24 min
   c 25 min   d 20 min

12. A factory employing 300 men assembles a given number of TV sets weekly, the number of working hours being 60 per week. How many men would be required for the same production, if the working hours are reduced to 40 per week?

   a 400   b 450
   c 500   d 300

13. Typing at 30 words per minute, Michael will be able to finish his essay in 2 h. His friend Michelle says that she should be able to finish it in one and a half hours. At what speed must she be able to type to do this?

   a 40   b 38
   c 42   d 45

14. A shopkeeper has first enough money to buy 50 fans worth ₹ 500 each. If each fan were to cost ₹ 20 more, then number of fans, he will able to buy with that amount of money (approx), is

   a 50   b 45
   c 48   d 40

15. In the festive season, company A launches an offer on his products. The offer is, you can buy either two watches or three fans in ₹ 1500. Ram wants to buy 6 fans and 6 watches. How much money he needs to buy this?

   a ₹ 10000   b ₹ 7500
   c ₹ 9000   d ₹ 10500

16. State 'T' for true or 'F' for false.

   I. When two quantities x and y are in direct proportion, then xy is constant.

   II. Length of a side of a square and its area are directly proportional to each other.

   III. If x and y are inversely proportional, then $(x + 1)$ and $(y + 1)$ are also in inverse proportion.

   IV. For a fixed time period and rate of interest, the simple interest is directly proportional to the principal.

Codes

	I	II	III	IV			I	II	III	IV
a	F	T	T	T		b	T	F	T	F
c	T	T	T	T		d	F	F	F	F

17. Fill in the blanks with the help of options, given in the box.

> (i) directly proportional, (ii) decreases, (iii) 8:15, (iv) no variation, (v) direct, (vi) increase, (vii) 15:8, (viii) indirect, (ix) 1:6, (x) 12:1

   I. The expenditure on petrol is ___ to the consumption.

   II. For $xy = 5$, if x increases, then y ___ .

   III. If $A : B = 2 : 3$, $B : C = 4 : 5$, then $A : C =$ ___ .

   IV.

x	90	60	45	30	20
y	10	5	2	25	30

   x and y follow ___ .

   V. If $\dfrac{1}{x} = \dfrac{x}{9}$ and $\dfrac{y}{2} = \dfrac{2}{16}$, then $x : y =$ ___ .

Codes

	I	II	III	IV	V
a	(v)	(ii)	(iii)	(iv)	(x)
b	(i)	(ii)	(iii)	(iv)	(x)
c	(viii)	(vii)	(vi)	(v)	(vi)
d	(iii)	(ii)	(i)	(iv)	(ix)

18. If 8 persons complete a piece of work in 6 days. Then, how many days it will take to complete the same work by 6 persons?

   a 12   b 8
   c 18   d 3

19. For a given job, more the number of workers, less will be time taken to complete the work. It is

   a direct proportion   b inverse proportion
   c ratio and proportion   d None of these

20. 60 cows graze a field in 15 days. How many cows will graze the field in 10 days?

    a 70   b 90   c 120   d 30

21. Dinesh goes to school at an average speed of 12 km/h and reach the school in 20 min. If he wants to reach his school in 15 min, then what should be his average speed?

    a 8 km/h   b 16 km/h

    c 12 km/h   d 20 km/h

22. Fill in the vacant place, regarding time and work problem.

Men	5	10	20	—	50
Time	20	10	—	4	2

    a 5, 20   b 5, 25

    c 20, 5   d 25, 10

23. A train covers a distance of 30 km in 30 min. How much time it will take to cover a distance of 15 km?

    a 1 h   b $\frac{1}{4}$ h   c $\frac{1}{3}$ h   d $\frac{1}{2}$ h

24. A man can complete $\frac{5}{8}$ of a job in 10 days.

At this rate, how many extra days will it take to complete $\frac{3}{4}$ of that job?

    a 12   b 16   c 2   d 6

25. If walking $\frac{4}{5}$ th of his usual speed, a person reaches in 20 min to his office, then what is his usual time to cover the distance?

    a 30 min   b 25 min

    c 45 min   d 1 h

26. A typist can type 3 pages containing 25 lines in each page in 2 h. The time, he will take to type 5 pages of 30 lines each, is

    a 2.30 h   b 3 h   c 3.30 h   d 4 h

27. If 10 men can do a work in 6 days and 15 women can do the same work in 6 days, then 8 men and 3 women together can do the same work in how many days?

    a 7   b 6   c 5   d 4

28. Two pipes can fill a tank in 30 min and 40 min respectively. Another pipe can empty the full tank in 20 min. If all the pipes are opened, when the tank is empty, then how much time it will take the fill the tank to $\frac{1}{2}$ of level?

    a 1 h   b 2 h   c 3 h   d $2\frac{1}{2}$ h

29. If a train 200 m long crosses a pole on the track in 10 min. Then, how much time will it take to cross a man standing in the opposite direction of pole?

    a 200 min   b 15 min

    c 10 min   d 30 min

30. State 'T' for true or 'F' for false.

    I. If the time duration increases in a journey of fixed distance, then its speed also increases.

    II. If a person can finish a job in 10 days, then the double of work by 2 persons can be finished in 10 days.

    III. Two persons can go to office at different speeds covering same distance, so they can reach office at same time, if they start travelling at same time.

    IV. In case of pipe and cistern, the water level of tank is directly proportional to the efficiency of the pipe.

Codes

	I	II	III	IV			I	II	III	IV
a	F	T	F	T		b	T	F	F	T
c	F	F	T	T		d	T	F	T	F

31. Fill in the blanks with the help of options, given in the box.

> (i) 15, (ii) 250, (iii) $\frac{1}{2}$, (iv) 2, (v) $\frac{1}{2}$,
> (vi) $\frac{1000}{6}$, (vii) 200, (viii) 12:30 pm,
> (ix) 100, (x) $12\frac{1}{2}$

    I. If $\frac{2}{5}$ th of a work is completed in 10 days the ___ days to complete $\frac{1}{2}$ of the work.

    II. If 30 dozens of eggs cost ₹ 600. Then, cost of 5 dozens of eggs is ___ .

    III. If 5 men or 10 women can complete a work in same time. Then, 1 man = ___ women.

    IV. If Divya travels 50 m distance in 75 steps. Then, the distance travelled in 375 steps is ___ m.

Codes

	I	II	III	IV
a	(x)	(ix)	(iv)	(ii)
b	(i)	(iii)	(iv)	(v)
c	(vi)	(viii)	(ix)	(x)
d	(xi)	(ii)	(iii)	(iv)

MATHEMATICS OLYMPIAD CLASS VIII

11
Quadrilaterals

1. Which of the following figures satisfies the property of having only one pair of parallel sides?

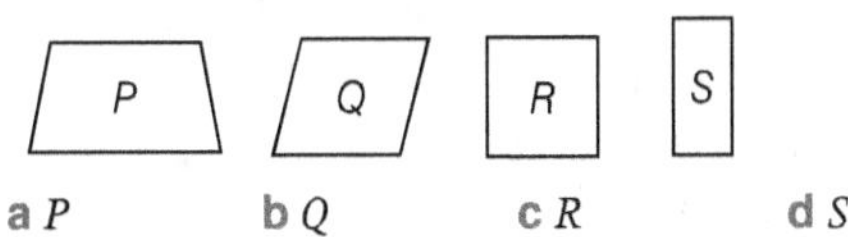

   a *P* b *Q* c *R* d *S*

2. Which of the following is a property of a parallelogram?
   a Opposite sides are parallel.
   b The diagonals bisect each other at right angles.
   c The diagonals are perpendicular to each other.
   d All angles are equal.

3. The maximum number of obtuse angles, a quadrilateral can have
   a 1   b 2
   c 3   d 4

4. In the trapezium given below, the measure of $\angle D$ is

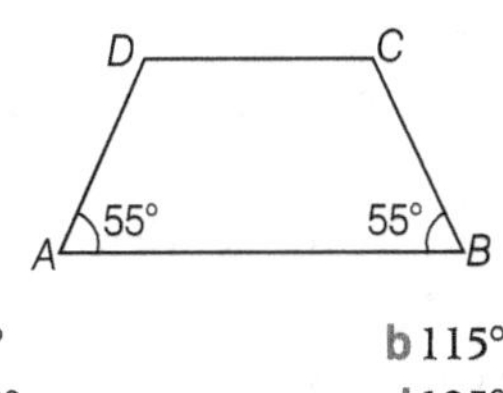

   a 55°   b 115°
   c 135°   d 125°

5. In the given figure, the value of $x + y + z + w$ is

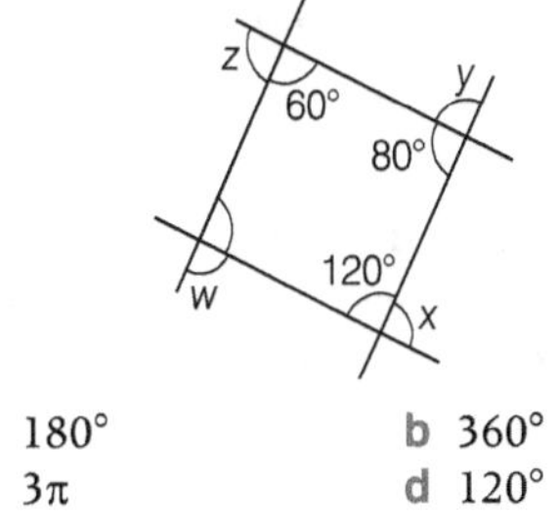

   a 180°   b 360°
   c 3π   d 120°

6. If the measures of two adjacent angles of a parallelogram are in the ratio 7 : 2, then the measures of all the angles of parallelogram are
   a 40°, 100°, 80°, 140°
   b 140°, 40°, 140°, 40°
   c 135°, 45°, 135°, 45°
   d 120°, 60°, 60°, 120°

7. The value of x in the given figure, of a parallelogram, is

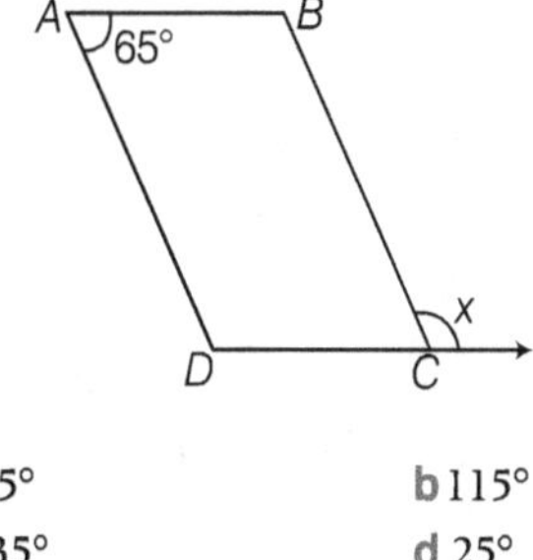

   a 65°   b 115°
   c 135°   d 25°

8. In the given trapezium, the value of x is

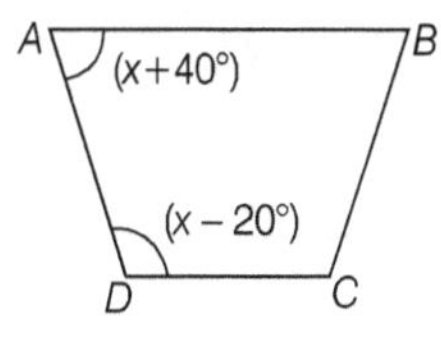

   a 80°   b 120°
   c 60°   d 90°

9. If two angles of a quadrilateral are 60° and 40° and the other two angles are in the ratio 16 : 10. Then, the measures of other two angles are
   a 80° and 50°   b 160° and 100°
   c 180° and 80°   d 120° and 140°

10. If the angles of a quadrilateral are in the ratio
   $1:2:3:4$, then which of the following is the
   greatest angle?

   a 142°

   b 124°

   c 144°

   d 200°

11. The adjacent angles of a parallelogram are
   $(2x-4)°$ and $(3x-1)°$. The measures of all
   angles of parallelogram are

   a 70°, 110°, 70°, 110°

   b 80°, 100°, 100°, 80°

   c 60°, 120°, 60°, 120°

   d None of the above

12. Match the following:

List I		List II
A.	Rectangle	i. All sides are equal.
B.	Square	ii. Opposite sides are equal and all angles are 90°.
C.	Rhombus	iii. All sides are equal and all angles are 90°.
D.	Trapezium	iv. One pair of opposite sides are parallel.

Codes

	A	B	C	D
a	(i)	(ii)	(iii)	(iv)
b	(ii)	(iii)	(i)	(iv)
c	(ii)	(i)	(iii)	(iv)
d	(iv)	(iii)	(ii)	(i)

13. $PQRS$ is a rectangle. If the perpendicular ST
   from S on PR divides $\angle S$ in the ratio $2:3$, then
   the measure of $\angle TPQ$ is

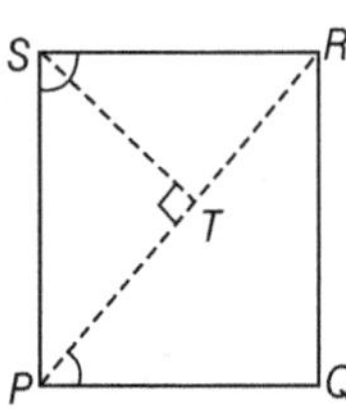

   a 54°

   b 36°

   c 90°

   d 18°

14. A playground in a town is in the form of a
   kite. The perimeter of playground is 106 m. If
   one of its sides is 23 m, then the length of
   other side is

   a 60 m

   b 30 m

   c 23 m

   d 46 m

15. In the parallelogram $PQRS$, O is the mid-point
   of SQ. Then, the ratio of $\angle S$ and $\angle R$ is

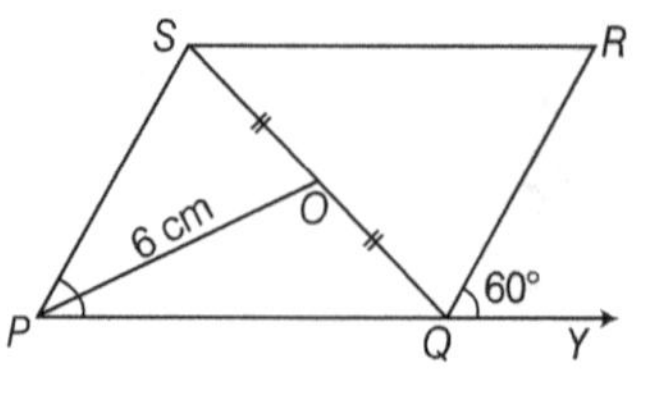

   a 1:2   b 2:1   c 1:3   d 3:1

16. If the measures of angles of a hexagon are $x°$,
   $(x-5)°$, $(x-5)°$, $(2x-5)°$, $(2x-5)°$ and $(2x+20)°$,
   then the value of x is

   a 60°   b 120°

   c 80°   d 90°

17. State 'T' for true or 'F' for false.

   I. A triangle which is an equilateral triangle
      may not be equiangular.

   II. All squares are rectangles.

   III. The sum of all exterior angles of a
      quadrilateral is 360°.

   IV. The angle sum property of a pentagon is
      $(5-2)\times180° = 540°$.

   V. The sum of all interior angles of n-sided
      polygon is $(2n-4)$ right angles.

Codes

	I	II	III	IV	V			I	II	III	IV	V
a	F	T	T	T	T		b	F	T	T	F	F
c	T	F	T	T	F		d	T	T	T	F	F

18. Fill in the blanks with the help of options,
   given in the box.

> (i) 60°, (ii) Square, (iii) 10, (iv) 12, (v) 90°,
> (vi) 6 cm, (vii) 12 cm, (viii) 120°, (ix) 120°,
> (x) Rectangle

   I. The measure of exterior angle of a regular
      hexagon is ___ .

   II. ___ is a regular quadrilateral.

   III. The number of sides of a regular polygon,
      where each exterior angle is 36°, is ___ .

   IV. In a rhombus, diagonals intersect at ___ .

   V. If length of one diagonal of a rectangle is
      6 cm, then the length of other diagonal is
      ___ .

Codes

	I	II	III	IV	V
a	(i)	(ii)	(iii)	(v)	(vi)
b	(ii)	(iii)	(iv)	(v)	(vi)
c	(vii)	(viii)	(ix)	(x)	(i)
d	(iv)	(v)	(vi)	(vii)	(i)

Practice
Sets

Practice Set 1

A Whole Content Based Test for Class 8th Mathematics Olympiad

1. The product of a rational number and its multiplicative inverse is always equal to
- a 0
- b -1
- c 1
- d its reciprocal

2. The value of m for given expression $3^m \div 3^{-3} = 3^4$ is
- a 6
- b 5
- c 1
- d 0

3. Which of the following numbers has no reciprocal?
- a 1
- b -1
- c 0
- d 5

4. The value of the given expression
$$\frac{7.25 \times 7.25 \times 7.25 + 1.75 \times 1.75 \times 1.75}{9}$$ is
- a 42.94
- b 40.42
- c 24.49
- d None of these

5. Simplify $\dfrac{\sqrt{441} + \sqrt{196}}{\sqrt{1024} - \sqrt{324}}$.
- a $\dfrac{2}{5}$
- b $\dfrac{2}{3}$
- c $\dfrac{5}{3}$
- d $\dfrac{5}{2}$

6. $\sqrt{41 - \sqrt{29 - \sqrt{18 - \sqrt{4}}}}$ is equivalent to
- a 2
- b 4
- c 6
- d 5

7. Which value of z for equation
$$z - \frac{z - 2 + 2z}{4} = 2z - \frac{4 + 3z}{2} \text{ is true?}$$
- a 4
- b 0
- c 10
- d 1

Direction (Q. No. 8) *Which of the following options is needed to answer the question?*
- a Only I is needed to answer the question
- b Both I and II are needed to answer the question
- c Only II is needed to answer the question
- d Either I or II is sufficient

8. How old is Rakesh?
  - I. Five years before, the age of Rakesh and his father was in ratio $1:3$.
  - II. Five years hence, sum of their ages will be 50 yr.

9. $RENT$ is a rectangle. Its diagonals meet at O. The value of x, if $OR = 2x + 4$ and $OT = 3x + 1$, is
- a 4
- b 3
- c 5
- d 6

10. Two numbers are in the ratio $4:5$. If sum of these two numbers is 27. Then, the product of numbers is
- a 190
- b 180
- c 225
- d 240

11. If the measure of two adjacent angles A and B of a parallelogram are in the ratio $3:2$, then the measure of the angle opposite to angle A is
- a $72°$
- b $108°$
- c $90°$
- d $144°$

12. One of the factors of the quotient when the polynomial $y^3 - 2y^2 - 9y + 18$ is divided by binomial $y - 2$.
- a $(y + 3)$
- b $(3 - y)$
- c $(2 - y)$
- d $(y^2 + 9)$

13. Sum of three numbers is 105. If the ratio between first and second numbers is $2:3$ and between second and third numbers is $4:5$. Then, the second number is
- a 35
- b 24
- c 36
- d 45

14. Evaluate and mark the correct option.
$$[(24^2 + 7^2)^{1/2}]^3$$
- a 625
- b 25
- c 1025
- d None of these

15. If $x * y = x + y - \sqrt{xy}$, then the value of $7 * 63$ is equal to
- a 63
- b 49
- c 21
- d 7

16. If $(2^{3x-1} + 10) \div 6 = 7$, then x is equal to

   a -2 b 0

   c 1 d 2

17. If a rational number is such that when we multiply it by $\dfrac{4}{5}$ and add $\dfrac{2}{3}$ of it to the product, we get $-\dfrac{11}{5}$. Then, the number is

   a $-\dfrac{1}{2}$ b $\dfrac{3}{2}$

   c $-\dfrac{3}{2}$ d $\dfrac{4}{5}$

18. In the given figure, if $ABCD$ is a rhombus and $\angle BCD = 80°$, then the values of x and y respectively are

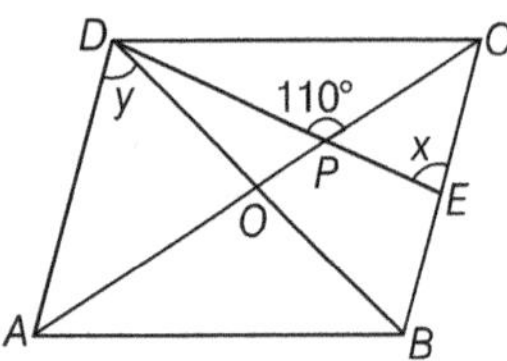

   a $42°$ and $20°$

   b $70°$ and $50°$

   c $80°$ and $30°$

   d $50°$ and $40°$

19. Which of the property of rational number is followed by the given expression?

$$\frac{4}{5}\left\{\frac{2}{5} - \frac{4}{5}\right\} = \frac{4}{5} \times \frac{2}{5} + \frac{4}{5} \times \left(-\frac{4}{5}\right)$$

   a Commutativity

   b Associativity

   c Distribution of multiplication over addition

   d All of the above

20. If $\dfrac{25 \times a^{-4}}{5^{-3} \times 10 \times a^{-8}} = x \times a^{4}$. Then, the value of x is

   a 5^3 b 5^4

   c $\dfrac{1}{2} \times 5^4$ d 5^2

21. The value of the expression $\dfrac{4z^2 - 9y^2}{2z + 3y}$ is

   a 1

   b 0

   c $4z + 9y$

   d $2z - 3y$

22. Sohan's father is 25 yr younger than Sohan's grandfather and 25 yr older than Sohan. The sum of the ages of all the three after 10 yr will be 180 yr. The present age of Sohan's grandfather is

   a 70 yr

   b 85 yr

   c 50 yr

   d 75 yr

23. A shopkeeper earns a profit of 12% after selling a book at 10% discount on printed price. Then, the ratio of the cost price and printed price of the book is

   a $45 : 56$

   b $50 : 61$

   c $99 : 125$

   d None of the above

Direction (Q. No. 24) *Which of the following options is needed to answer the question?*

   a Only I is needed to answer the question

   b Both I and II are needed to answer the question

   c Only II is needed to answer the question

   d Either I or II is sufficient

24. How much time it will be taken by the train to cross a person standing on the platform, if

   I. speed to train is 60 km/h and it crosses a bridge of equal length in 1 min?

   II. it also crosses a train coming from opposite direction in 45 s?

25. If $z = 6$, then the value of $20z\sqrt{z^3 - 2z^2}$ is

   a 1000 b 1040

   c 1400 d 1440

26. For how many 3-digit perfect cubes, the sum of the digits is not a perfect square?

   a 1 b 2

   c 3 d 4

27. If 4 men or 8 women can complete a work in 8 days. A contractor starts working with 6 women and 1 man and due to some emergency he need to complete the work in 4 days. How much more men he needed?

   a 4 b 3

   c 6 d 8

Practice Set 1

28. The value of expression $\dfrac{-\sqrt{\left(\dfrac{5}{3}\right)^2 \times \left(\dfrac{3}{5}\right)^2}}{-\sqrt{\left(\dfrac{2}{5}\right)^3 \times \left(\dfrac{2}{5}\right)^{-3}}}$ is

   a 1   **b** -1

   c 2   **d** $\dfrac{25}{6}$

29. An expression is to be written in the form of $x^2 - (a + b)x + ab$, where a and b, $(a, b > 0)$ are such that sum of their squares is 20 and difference of their squares is 12. The expression is

   a $x^2 + 6x - 12$ **b** $x^2 - 6x + 8$

   c $x^2 - 8x + 12$ **d** $x^2 - 8x + 16$

30. In the given figure, if *RISK* and *CLUE* are parallelograms. Then, the value of x is

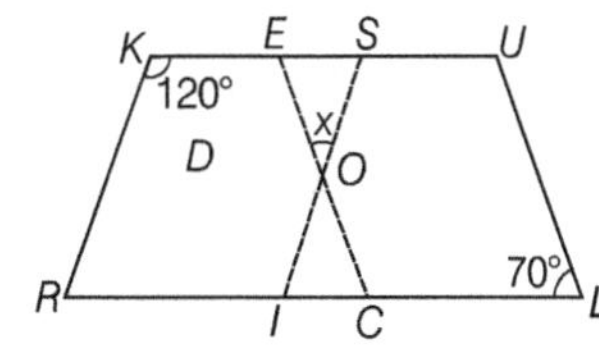

   a 50°

   b 60°

   c 80°

   d 70°

Solutions

1. (c) Let $\dfrac{a}{b}$ be the rational number.

∴ Its multiplicative inverse $= \dfrac{b}{a}$

So, we have $\dfrac{a}{b} \times \dfrac{b}{a} = 1$

2. (c) $3^m \div 3^{-3} = 3^4$

$\Rightarrow \qquad 3^m = 3^4 \times 3^{-3}$

$\Rightarrow \qquad 3^m = 3^1$

$\Rightarrow \qquad m = 1 \qquad$ [by comparing]

3. (c) 0 has no reciprocal.

4. (a) Given $\dfrac{7.25 \times 7.25 \times 7.25 + 1.75 \times 1.75 \times 1.75}{9}$

$= \dfrac{(7.25)^3 + (1.75)^3}{9}$

Using identity, $(a^3 + b^3) = (a + b)(a^2 + b^2 - ab)$

$= \dfrac{(7.25 + 1.75)\,[(7.25)^2 + (1.75)^2 - (7.25)(1.75)]}{9}$

$= \dfrac{9\,(52.56 + 3.06 - 12.68)}{9} = 42.94$

5. (d) Consider,

$\dfrac{\sqrt{441} + \sqrt{196}}{\sqrt{1024} - \sqrt{324}} = \dfrac{21 + 14}{32 - 18} = \dfrac{35}{14} = \dfrac{5}{2}$

6. (c) Consider,

$\sqrt{41 - \sqrt{29 - \sqrt{18 - \sqrt{4}}}}$

$= \sqrt{41 - \sqrt{29 - \sqrt{18 - 2}}}$

$= \sqrt{41 - \sqrt{29 - \sqrt{16}}} = \sqrt{41 - \sqrt{29 - 4}}$

$= \sqrt{41 - \sqrt{25}} = \sqrt{41 - 5} = \sqrt{36} = 6$

7. (c) Given, $z - \dfrac{z - 2 + 2z}{4} = 2z - \dfrac{4 + 3z}{2}$

$(4z - z + 2 - 2z)\,2 = (4z - 4 - 3z)\,4$

$\Rightarrow \qquad (z + 2)\,2 = (z - 4)\,4$

$\Rightarrow \qquad 2z + 4 = 4z - 16$

$\Rightarrow \qquad 4 + 16 = 4z - 2z$

$\Rightarrow \qquad 20 = 2z \Rightarrow z = 10$

8. (b)

9. (b) Given, *RENT* is a rectangle with diagonals *RN* and *ET*.
Now, since diagonals of a rectangle are equal and bisect each other.

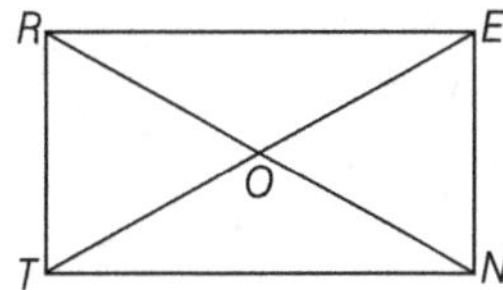

∴ $2x + 4 = 3x + 1 \Rightarrow x = 3$

10. (b) Given, $\qquad \dfrac{a}{b} = \dfrac{4}{5} \qquad$ ... (i)

and $\qquad a + b = 27 \qquad$ ... (ii)

From Eqs. (i) and (ii), we get

$\dfrac{4}{5}b + b = 27 \Rightarrow \dfrac{9}{5}b = 27 \Rightarrow b = 15$

∴ $\qquad a = 12$

So, $a \times b = 15 \times 12 = 180$

11. (b) Let angles be $3x$ and $2x$.

Then, $3x + 2x = 180° \Rightarrow x = 36°$

∴ Angle opposite to $\angle A = 3x = 3 \times 36° = 108°$

12. (a) Consider, $y^3 - 2y^2 - 9y + 18$

$= y^2(y - 2) - 9(y - 2)$

$= (y^2 - 9)(y - 2)$

So, $\qquad \dfrac{y^3 - 2y^2 - 9y + 18}{y - 2} = \dfrac{(y^2 - 9)\,(y - 2)}{y - 2}$

$= y^2 - 9 = (y - 3)\,(y + 3)$

13. (c) Let the three numbers be a, b and c.

According to the question,

$a + b + c = 105$

$\dfrac{a}{b} = \dfrac{2}{3}$ and $\dfrac{b}{c} = \dfrac{4}{5}$

We have,

$b = \dfrac{4}{5}c$

Practice Set 1

Also,
$$\frac{a}{b} \times \frac{b}{c} = \frac{2}{3} \times \frac{4}{5}$$
$$\Rightarrow \quad \frac{a}{c} = \frac{8}{15}$$
$$\therefore \quad a = \frac{8}{15}c$$

So, we have
$$\frac{8}{15}c + \frac{4}{5}c + c = 105$$
$$\Rightarrow \quad 8c + 12c + 15c = 105 \times 15$$
$$\Rightarrow \quad 35c = 105 \times 15$$
$$\Rightarrow \quad c = 3 \times 15 = 45$$
So,
$$b = \frac{4}{5} \times 45 = 36$$

14. (d) Consider,
$$[(24^2 + 7^2)^{1/2}]^3 = [(625)^{1/2}]^3$$
$$= [25]^3 = 15625$$

15. (b) Given $x * y = x + y - \sqrt{xy}$
$$\therefore \quad 7 * 63 = 7 + 63 - \sqrt{7 \times 63} = 70 - 21 = 49$$

16. (d) $(2^{3x-1} + 10) \div 6 = 7$
$$\Rightarrow \quad 2^{3x-1} + 10 = 7 \times 6$$
$$\Rightarrow \quad 2^{3x-1} = 42 - 10$$
$$\Rightarrow \quad 2^{3x-1} = 2^5 [$$
$$\because 32 = 2^5]$$
$$\Rightarrow \quad 3x - 1 = 5 \qquad \text{[by comparing]}$$
$$\Rightarrow \quad 3x = 6 \Rightarrow x = 2$$

17. (c) Let the number be x.
According to the question, $\frac{4}{5}x + \frac{2}{3}x = \frac{-11}{5}$
$$\Rightarrow \quad \frac{12x + 10x}{15} = \frac{-11}{5} \Rightarrow \frac{22x}{3} = -11$$
$$\Rightarrow \quad x = -\frac{3}{2}$$

18. (b) Given, $\angle DPC = 110°$ and $\angle BCD = 80°$

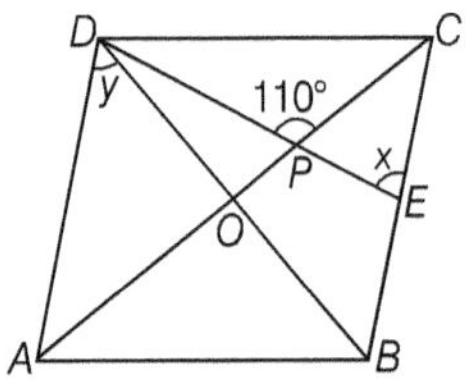

In ΔDOP,
$$\angle DOP + \angle ODP = 110° \qquad \text{[exterior angle theorem]}$$
$$\therefore 90° + \angle ODP = 110° \qquad \text{[diagonals of rhombus intersect}$$
$$\text{each other at } 90°]$$
$$\therefore \angle ODP = 20°$$
Now, $AD \parallel BC$ and DE is the transversal.
$$\because \qquad \angle x = \angle y + 20°$$
From the given options, only option (b) satisfies the relation.

19. (c)

20. (c) $\dfrac{25 \times a^{-4}}{5^{-3} \times 10 \times a^{-8}} = x \times a^4$
$$\Rightarrow \quad \frac{(5)^2}{5^{-3} \times 5 \times 2} \times a^4 = x \times a^4$$
$$\Rightarrow \quad \frac{5^{2+3-1}}{2} \times a^4 = x \times a^4$$
$$\Rightarrow \quad \frac{1}{2} \times 5^4 \times a^4 = x \times a^4$$
$$\Rightarrow \quad x = \frac{1}{2} \times 5^4$$

21. (d) Consider, $\dfrac{4z^2 - 9y^2}{2z + 3y}$
$$= \frac{(2z)^2 - (3y)^2}{(2z + 3y)} = \frac{(2z - 3y)(2z + 3y)}{(2z + 3y)} = 2z - 3y$$

22. (d) Let present age of Sohan's grandfather be x yr.
Then, age of father $= (x - 25)$ yr
and age of Sohan $= (x - 25) - 25$ yr
According to the question,
After 10 yr,
$$(x + 10) + (x - 25 + 10) + (x - 25 - 25 + 10) = 180$$
$$\Rightarrow \quad 3x + (10 - 25 + 10 - 50 + 10) = 180$$
$$\Rightarrow \quad 3x + (30 - 75) = 180$$
$$\Rightarrow \quad 3x - 45 = 180$$
$$\Rightarrow \quad 3x = 180 + 45 \Rightarrow 3x = 225$$
$$\therefore \quad x = \frac{225}{3} = 75$$

Hence, the present age of Sohan's grandfather is 75 yr.

23. (a) Let printed price be ₹ 100.
Then, SP after 10% discount $= ₹ (100 - 10) = ₹ 90$
Profit per cent earned 12%
CP of article $= ₹ \dfrac{100}{112} \times 90 = ₹ \dfrac{1125}{14}$
$\therefore$ Ratio of CP : Printed price $= \dfrac{1125}{14} : 100 = 45 : 56$

24. (a)

25. (d) Consider, $20z\sqrt{z^3 - 2z^2}$
$$= 20z \times z\sqrt{z - 2} = 20 \times 36 \times \sqrt{6 - 2}$$
$$= 20 \times 36 \times 2 = 1440$$

26. (d) 3-digit perfect cubes are 125, 216, 343, 512, 729.
Only sum of digits of 125 is a perfect cube $\quad (= 8)$.

27. (a) 4 men = 8 women
$$\Rightarrow 1 \text{ man} = 2 \text{ women}$$
So, we have
6 women + 1 man = 6 women + 2 women = 8 women
8 women complete work in 8 days.
To complete work in 4 days, number of women required
$$= \frac{8 \times 8}{4} = 16 \text{ women}$$
$$\Rightarrow 16 \text{ women} = 6 \text{ women} + 10 \text{ women}$$
$$= 6 \text{ women} + 5 \text{ men}$$
$\therefore$ Number of extra men $= 5 - 1 = 4$

28. (a) Consider, $\dfrac{-\sqrt{\left(\frac{5}{3}\right)^2 \times \left(\frac{3}{5}\right)^2}}{-\sqrt{\left(\frac{2}{5}\right)^3 \times \left(\frac{2}{5}\right)^{-3}}} = \dfrac{-\sqrt{\left(\frac{5}{3}\right)^{2-2}}}{-\sqrt{\left(\frac{2}{5}\right)^{3-3}}} = \dfrac{-1}{-1} = 1$

29. (b) Given, $x^2 - (a + b)x + ab$
$$a^2 + b^2 = 20 \qquad \text{[given]}$$
and $\qquad a^2 - b^2 = 12 \qquad \text{[given]}$
On solving above equations, we get
$$a = 4, b = 2 \qquad \text{[where, } a, b > 0]$$
$\therefore$ Expression $= x^2 - 6x + 8$

30. (a) In parallelogram $RISK$, $\angle K = 120°$
$$\therefore \angle R = 180° - 120° = 60°$$
$$\angle S = \angle R = 60°$$
and in parallelogram $CLUE$,
$$\angle L = \angle E = 70°$$
In ΔOES, $\angle E + \angle S + \angle O = 180°$
$$\Rightarrow \quad 70° + 60° + \angle O = 180°$$
$$\Rightarrow \quad 130° + x = 180°$$
$$\therefore \quad x = 50°$$

Practice Set 2

A Whole Content Based Test for Class 8th Mathematics Olympiad

1. Which of the following rational numbers lies between 0 and 1?

  a $\dfrac{1}{2}, \dfrac{25}{26}, \dfrac{50}{101}$ b $\dfrac{4}{5}, \dfrac{8}{7}, \dfrac{6}{5}$

  c $\dfrac{14}{15}, \dfrac{16}{9}, \dfrac{5}{9}$ d None of these

2. The factors of $x^8 - 625$ is

  a $x^4 + 5$ b $x^2 + 5$

  c $x^4 + 25$ d Both (b) and (c)

3. Solution of the equation $x - \dfrac{x+1}{4} = 2 - \dfrac{x-3}{3}$ is

  a $\dfrac{13}{3}$ b 3   c -3 d 15

4. Hitesh is 40 yr old and Rohit is 60 yr old. How many years ago, the ratio of their ages was $3:5$?

  a 10   b 20   c 15   d 25

5. $ABCD$ is a parallelogram, given in the figure. It is also given that, $OB = 4$ and AC is 5 more than BD. The value of OA is

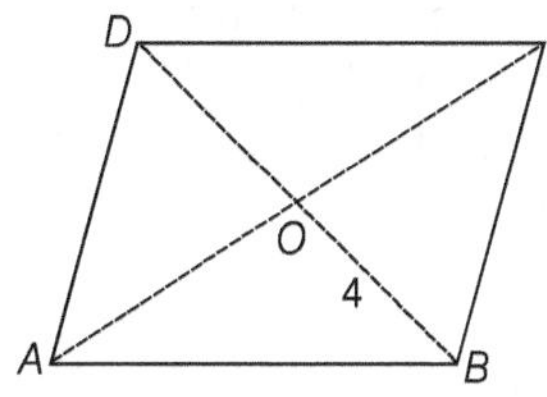

  a 13   b 6.5   c 7   d 9

6. The value of the expression $\dfrac{2}{5} \times \dfrac{5}{2} - \dfrac{2}{5} \times \dfrac{5}{4}$ is

  a 0   b 1

  c $\dfrac{1}{2}$ d -1

7. The value of x, if $(x)^{1/2} = 2 \times (x)^{1/3}$, is

  a 26   b 64

  c 216   d 128

8. Which of the following is not a factor of expression $(2a + b)^2 - (3a - b)^2$?

  a 1   b $5a$

  c $a + 2b$ d $-a + 2b$

9. The square root of
$$\dfrac{(0.25)^3}{(1-0.25)^2} + \left[\dfrac{0.25 + (0.25)^2 + 1}{(1-0.25)}\right] \text{ is}$$

  a 1   b 2

  c 5   d None of these

10. If $p * q = p - q + \sqrt{pq}$, then $18 * 8$ is equal to

  a 20   b 22   c 24   d 10

11. Sum of the digits of a 2-digit number is 11. When we interchange the digits, it is found that the resulting new number is greater than the original number by 27. What is new number?

  a 74   b 92   c 47   d 65

12. Rahul can do a piece of work in 20 days. Mohan is doing same work 25% more efficiently than Rahul. If both together start working, then in how many days they complete the work?

  a 15   b 25

  c $\dfrac{80}{9}$ d $\dfrac{100}{9}$

13. The value of y for given expression
$$\left(\dfrac{5}{3}\right)^{-4} \times \left(\dfrac{5}{3}\right)^{-5} = \left(\dfrac{5}{3}\right)^{3y} \times \left(\dfrac{5}{3}\right)^{0} \text{ is}$$

  a 3   b -3 c 0   d -1

14. The value of $\sqrt{\dfrac{(0.02)^2 + (0.18)^2 + (0.42)^2}{(0.002)^2 + (0.018)^2 + (0.042)^2}}$ is

  a 0.1   b 10   c 10^2 d 10^3

15. The polynomial $p(x) = x^3 - 4x - 15$, when divided by the binomial $(x - 3)$, we get remainder as

  a 1   b 2   c 0   d -1

16. Three consecutive integers are such that when they are taken in decreasing order and multiplied by 5, 6 and 7 respectively, they add upto 214. The average of the numbers is

  a 11   b 12   c 10   d 9

17. The profit earned by selling an article for ₹ 317 is equal to loss incurred when the same article is sold for ₹ 233. The SP of article in order to gain of 20% is

   a ₹ 390   b ₹ 370
   c ₹ 350   d ₹ 330

18. If the ratio between exterior angle and interior angle of a regular polygon is $1:5$, then the number of sides of polygon is

   a 5   b 8   c 12   d 10

19. Which of the following statements is false?

   a 0 is a rational number
   b All natural numbers are not necessarily rational numbers
   c Rational numbers are always integers.
   d Both (b) and (c)

20. Divya purchased 11 books for ₹ 10 and sold all books at the rate of 10 for ₹ 11. Then, profit/loss per cent is

   a 10%   b 11%
   c 21%   d 100%

21. If $\left(\dfrac{2}{3}\right)$rd of a number is multiplied by $\dfrac{3}{4}$, the resulting number is 6. Then, the number is

   a 9   b 12   c 36   d 54

22. Simplify $\sqrt{\dfrac{(0.0144)\times(0.0289)}{(0.0025)\times(0.0441)}}$.

   a $\dfrac{12}{31}$ b $\dfrac{64}{39}$ c 60   d $\dfrac{68}{35}$

23. Rekha working 4 h a day typing 30 pages in a day, completes a project in 40 days. If she starts working 5 h a day, how many days she will take to complete the project?

   a 18   b 24   c 30   d 40

24. Which of the following steps in calculation of compound interest is wrong?

   I. $P = ₹\,10000,\ r = 10\%,\ t = 1\dfrac{1}{2}$ yr compounded half-yearly

   II. $A = P\left(1+\dfrac{r}{100}\right)^{n}$

   III. $n = 3,\ r = 10\%$

   IV. $A = ₹\,10000\left(1+\dfrac{10}{100}\right)^{3}$

   V. $CI = A - P = ₹\,1576.2$

   a II   b Both III and IV
   c IV   d Both IV and V

25. Two persons A and B walking on a circular track as shown in figure. Both have different speeds. If A completes one round in 5 min and B in 10 min. If both travelling in opposite direction, then how much time, it will take to complete the distance?

   a 4 min   b 6 min
   c $\dfrac{10}{3}$ min   d 5 min

26. If a field is in the form of a quadrilateral and the two lines joining opposite vertex are bisecting the vertex angle and also they intersect each other at right angle but the length of the two lines are different. Then, the type of the field is

   a rectangle   b square
   c rhombus   d parallelogram

27. Sanju has currency notes of denominations ₹ 100, ₹ 500 and ₹ 1000, respectively. The ratio of the number of these notes is $2:3:5$. The total cash with Sanju is ₹ 20100. How many notes of ₹ 500 denomination does he have?

   a 2   b 6   c 9   d 15

28. Ajay wants to mix the flour of two different rates, so that he can sell at the rate he wants. In what proportion, he must mix the flour at ₹ 16.6 per kg with a flour at ₹ 16.45 per kg, so that the mixture can be sold at the rate of ₹ 16.54 per kg?

   a $1:3$ b $2:3$
   c $1:2$ d $3:2$

29. If $\dfrac{a}{b}=\dfrac{4}{3}$, find the value of $\dfrac{a^2+b^2}{a^2-b^2}$.

   a $\dfrac{25}{7}$ b $\dfrac{26}{7}$
   c $\dfrac{25}{4}$ d 4

30. Manish borrowed a sum of ₹ 2000 at 20% per annum at compound interest compounded half-yearly. Immediately, he lends it another person at the same rate on the condition that the interest is compounded for every $\dfrac{1}{4}$th year. The amount gained by Manish in 1 yr is

   a ₹ 11.01   b ₹ 12.02
   c ₹ 13.03   d ₹ 14.04

Practice Set 2

Solutions

1. (a)

2. (d) $x^8 - 625$

$$= (x^4)^2 - (25)^2 = (x^4 + 25)(x^4 - 25)$$
$$= (x^4 + 25)[(x^2)^2 - (5)^2] = (x^4 + 25)[(x^2 + 5)(x^2 - 5)]$$
$$[\because a^2 - b^2 = (a + b)(a - b)]$$

3. (b) Consider

$$x - \frac{x + 1}{4} = 2 - \frac{x - 3}{3}$$
$$\Rightarrow \quad \frac{4x - x - 1}{4} = \frac{6 - x + 3}{3}$$
$$\Rightarrow \quad \frac{3x - 1}{4} = \frac{9 - x}{3}$$
$$\Rightarrow \quad 9x - 3 = 36 - 4x$$
$$\Rightarrow \quad 13x = 39$$
$$\therefore \quad x = \frac{39}{13} = 3$$

4. (a) Let x years ago, the ratio of their ages = $3 : 5$.

$$\therefore \quad \frac{40 - x}{60 - x} = \frac{3}{5} \Rightarrow 200 - 5x = 180 - 3x$$
$$\Rightarrow \quad 2x = 20 \Rightarrow x = 10$$

5. (b) $AC = BD + 5$ [given]

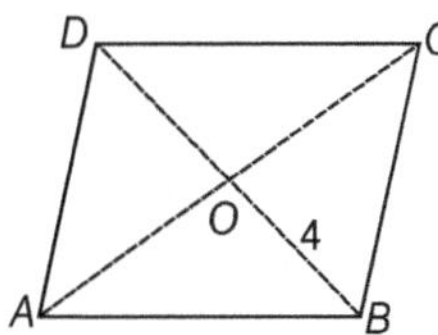

$\because$ Diagonals of a parallelogram bisect each other.

$$\therefore \quad OA = OC \text{ and } OB = OD$$
$$\therefore \quad BD = 4 + 4 = 8$$

Also, $\quad AC = OA + OC = 8 + 5 = 13$

$$\therefore \quad OA = \frac{13}{2} = 6.5$$

6. (c) We have, $\dfrac{2}{5} \times \dfrac{5}{2} - \dfrac{2}{5} \times \dfrac{5}{4} = 1 - \dfrac{1}{2} = \dfrac{1}{2}$

7. (b) $(x)^{1/2} = 2 \times (x)^{1/3}$

$$\Rightarrow \quad \frac{x^{1/2}}{x^{1/3}} = 2 \Rightarrow x^{1/2 - 1/3} = 2$$
$$\Rightarrow \quad x^{1/6} = 2 \Rightarrow x = 2^6 = 64$$

8. (c) We have, $(2a + b)^2 - (3a - b)^2$

$$= [\{(2a + b) + (3a - b)\} \{2a + b - 3a + b\}]$$
$$= 5a \times (2b - a)$$

9. (d) We have,

$$\sqrt{\frac{(0.25)^3}{(1 - 0.25)^2} + \frac{[(0.25) + (0.25)^2 + 1]}{(1 - 0.25)}}$$

$$= \sqrt{\frac{(0.25)^3 + (1 - 0.25)[(0.25) + (0.25)^2 + 1]}{(0.75)(0.75)}}$$

$$= \sqrt{\frac{(0.25)^3 + [1^3 - (0.25)^3]}{(0.75)(0.75)}}$$

$$= \frac{1}{0.75} = \frac{100}{75} = \frac{4}{3}$$

10. (b) Given, $p * q = p - q + \sqrt{pq}$

$$\therefore \quad 18 * 8 = 18 - 8 + \sqrt{18 \times 8}$$
$$= 10 + \sqrt{144} = 10 + 12 = 22$$

11. (a) Let the digit at ten's place be x.

Original number $= 10x + (11 - x)$

So, new number $= (11 - x) \times 10 + x$

According to the question,

$$(110 - 10x + x) - (10x + 11 - x) = 27$$
$$\Rightarrow \quad 110 - 9x - 9x - 11 = 27$$
$$\Rightarrow \quad 99 - 18x = 27$$
$$\Rightarrow \quad 99 - 27 = 18x$$
$$\Rightarrow \quad 72 = 18x$$
$$\therefore \quad x = 4$$

Hence, new number $= (11 - 4) \times 10 + 4$
$$= 70 + 4 = 74$$

12. (c) Number of days Rahul takes $= 20$ days

$\because$ Mohan is 25% more efficient.

$$\therefore \text{ Time taken by Mohan} = 16 \text{ days} \left[\because 20 \times \frac{100}{125} \right]$$

Now, total work in 1 day $= \dfrac{1}{20} + \dfrac{1}{16} = \dfrac{9}{80}$

$$\therefore \text{ Time taken to complete the work} = \frac{80}{9} \text{ days}$$

13. (b) We have, $\left(\dfrac{5}{3}\right)^{-4} \times \left(\dfrac{5}{3}\right)^{-5} = \left(\dfrac{5}{3}\right)^{3y} \times \left(\dfrac{5}{3}\right)^{0}$

$$\Rightarrow \quad \left(\frac{5}{3}\right)^{-4-5} = \left(\frac{5}{3}\right)^{3y} \times 1$$
$$\Rightarrow \quad -9 = 3y \qquad \text{[by comparing]}$$
$$\Rightarrow \quad y = -3$$

14. (b) We have,

$$\sqrt{\frac{(0.02)^2 + (0.18)^2 + (0.42)^2}{(0.002)^2 + (0.018)^2 + (0.042)^2}}$$

$$= \sqrt{\frac{\left(\frac{2}{100}\right)^2 + \left(\frac{18}{100}\right)^2 + \left(\frac{42}{100}\right)^2}{\left(\frac{2}{1000}\right)^2 + \left(\frac{18}{1000}\right)^2 + \left(\frac{42}{1000}\right)^2}}$$

$$= \sqrt{\frac{[(2)^2 + (18)^2 + (42)^2]}{[(2)^2 + (18)^2 + (42)^2]} \times \frac{(1000)^2}{(100)^2}}$$

$$= \frac{1000}{100} = 10$$

15. (c) Consider $(x^3 - 4x - 15) \div (x - 3)$

$$
\begin{array}{r}
x^2 + 3x + 5 \\
x - 3 \overline{\smash{)}\ x^3 - 4x - 15} \\
\underline{x^3 - 3x^2} \\
-\ \ + \\
\underline{3x^2 - 4x - 15} \\
3x^2 - 9x \\
\underline{-\ \ +} \\
5x - 15 \\
\underline{5x - 15} \\
0
\end{array}
$$

Practice Set 2

16. (b) Let three consecutive integers be $x, (x+1)$ and $(x+2)$ when taken in decreasing order and multiplied by 5, 6 and 7, respectively.

According to the question,
$$5(x+2) + 6(x+1) + 7x = 214$$
$$\Rightarrow \quad 5x + 10 + 6x + 6 + 7x = 214$$
$$\Rightarrow \quad 18x + 16 = 214$$
$$\Rightarrow \quad 18x = 198$$
$$\Rightarrow \quad x = \frac{198}{18}$$
$$\Rightarrow \quad x = 11$$

$\therefore$ Numbers are 11, 12 and 13.

So, average of the numbers $= \dfrac{11+12+13}{3} = \dfrac{36}{3} = 12$

17. (d) Let CP of article be x.

According to the question,
$$317 - x = x - 233$$
$$\Rightarrow \quad 2x = 550 \Rightarrow x = ₹275$$
CP of article $= ₹\,275$

Profit per cent $= 20\%$ [given]

$\therefore$ New SP $= 275 \times \dfrac{120}{100} = ₹\,330$

18. (c) $\dfrac{(n-2) \times 180°}{360°} = \dfrac{5}{1}$

$\Rightarrow \quad n - 2 = 10 \Rightarrow n = 12$

19. (d)

20. (c) CP of 11 books $= ₹\,10$

SP of 10 books $= ₹\,11$

CP of 110 books $= ₹\,10 \times 10 = ₹\,100$

SP of 110 books $= ₹\,11 \times 11 = ₹\,121$

Profit $= ₹\,(121 - 100) = ₹\,21$

$\therefore$ Profit per cent $= \dfrac{21}{100} \times 100 = 21\%$

Alternative method

By unit formula,

Profit per cent $= \dfrac{11^2 - 10^2}{10^2} \times 100 = 21\%$

21. (b) Let the number be x.

According to the question,
$$\left(\frac{2}{3}\right) x \times \frac{3}{4} = 6$$
$$\Rightarrow \quad \frac{6}{12} x = 6 \Rightarrow x = \frac{6 \times 12}{6}$$
$$\therefore \quad x = 12$$

22. (d) We have, $\sqrt{\dfrac{(0.0144) \times (0.0289)}{(0.0025) \times (0.0441)}}$

$$= \sqrt{\frac{(0.12)^2 \times (0.17)^2}{(0.05)^2 \times (0.21)^2}} = \frac{0.12 \times 0.17}{0.05 \times 0.21}$$

$$= \frac{12 \times 17}{5 \times 21} = \frac{4 \times 17}{5 \times 7} = \frac{68}{35}$$

23. (b) Let the number of pages be x.

$\therefore$ We have, $4 \times 30 \times 40 = 5 \times x \times 40$

$\Rightarrow x = 24$

24. (b) Here, $n = 3$, $r = \dfrac{10}{2} = 5\%$

$\because$ Interest compounded half-yearly.

$\therefore$ Steps III and IV both are wrong.

25. (c) Radius of circle $= 28\,\text{m}$

$\therefore$ Circumference $= 2 \times \dfrac{22}{7} \times 28\,\text{m} = 176\,\text{m}$

Speed of $A = \dfrac{176}{5}$ m/min

Speed of $B = \dfrac{176}{10}$ m/min

When they are in opposite direction, then

Net speed $= \dfrac{176}{5} + \dfrac{176}{10} = \dfrac{528}{10}$ m/min

$\therefore$ Time taken $= \dfrac{176}{528} \times 10 = \dfrac{10}{3}$ min

26. (c)

27. (c) Let the number of notes be x.

According to the question,
$$2x \times 100 + 3x \times 500 + 5x \times 1000 = 20100$$
$$\Rightarrow \quad 200x + 1500x + 5000x = 20100$$
$$\Rightarrow \quad 6700x = 20100$$
$$\Rightarrow \quad x = 3$$

Hence, number of ₹ 500 denomination $= 3 \times 3 = 9$

28. (d) Use alligation rule,

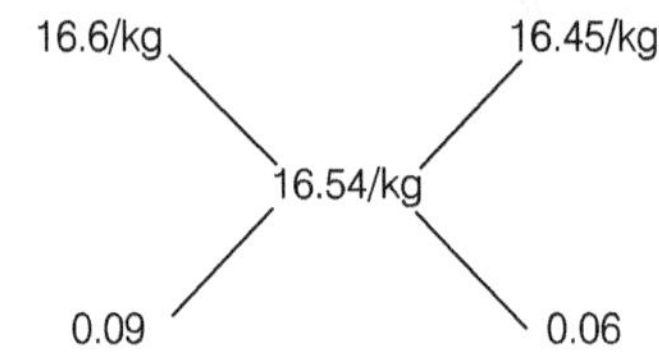

$\therefore$ Required ratio $= \dfrac{0.09}{0.06} = \dfrac{3}{2} = 3:2$

29. (a) Given, $\dfrac{a}{b} = \dfrac{4}{3}$

Consider $\dfrac{a^2 + b^2}{a^2 - b^2}$

$$= \frac{\left(\dfrac{a}{b}\right)^2 + 1}{\left(\dfrac{a}{b}\right)^2 - 1} = \frac{\left(\dfrac{4}{3}\right)^2 + 1}{\left(\dfrac{4}{3}\right)^2 - 1}$$

$$= \frac{\dfrac{16+9}{9}}{\dfrac{16-9}{9}} = \frac{25}{7}$$

30. (a) Money paid by Manish $= 2000\left(1 + \dfrac{10}{100}\right)^2$

$$= 2000\left(\frac{11}{10}\right)\left(\frac{11}{10}\right) = 121 \times 20 = ₹\,2420$$

Money received by Manish $= 2000\left(1 + \dfrac{5}{100}\right)^4$

$$= 2000\left(\frac{21}{20}\right)^4$$

$$= 2000 \times \frac{21 \times 21 \times 21 \times 21}{20 \times 20 \times 20 \times 20}$$

$$= ₹\,2431.01$$

$\therefore$ Amount gained by Manish

$$= ₹\,2431.01 - ₹\,2420$$
$$= ₹\,11.01$$

Practice Set 2

Practice Set ③

A Whole Content Based Test for Class 8th Mathematics Olympiad

1. The ratio which $\left(\dfrac{1}{3}\text{ of }₹9.30\right)$ is to $(0.6\text{ of }₹1.55)$ is

   a $1:3$ b $10:3$ c $3:10$ d $3:1$

2. Which of the following is additive inverse of $\dfrac{250}{625}$?

   a $\dfrac{625}{250}$ b $-\dfrac{625}{250}$ c $-\dfrac{2}{5}$ d 0

3. The value of expression $\left(\dfrac{9}{5}\right)^2 \times \left(\dfrac{3}{5}\right)^{-2} \times \left(\dfrac{5}{3}\right)^0$ is

   a 10 b 9 c 20 d 30

4. The value of x in the expression $28\sqrt{x}+1426=\dfrac{3}{4}$ of 2872 is

   a 576 b 676 c 1296 d 1444

5. What number should be added to 2200 to make it a perfect square?

   a 12 b 4 c 9 d 25

6. If $y+\dfrac{1}{y}=9$, then the value of the expression $y^3+\dfrac{1}{y^3}/y^2+\dfrac{1}{y^2}$ will be

   a $\dfrac{79}{702}$ b $\dfrac{702}{79}$ c $\dfrac{702}{790}$ d $\dfrac{790}{702}$

7. If two numbers x and y are such that $x:y=2:3,\ 2:x=1:2$. Then, the value of y is

   a 4 b 6 c $\dfrac{1}{3}$ d $\dfrac{3}{2}$

8. Three persons age are in the ratio $1:2:3$. If sum of youngest and eldest is 60 yr and that of middle and youngest is 45 yr. The age of eldest person will be

   a 50 yr   b 45 yr   c 40 yr   d 30 yr

9. If three angles of a quadrilateral are equal. Fourth angle is of measure $120°$, then the value of equal angle is

   a $80°$ b $90°$ c $110°$ d $60°$

10. If $(-x)$ is the additive inverse of x, then additive inverse of $-\dfrac{1}{5}$ is

   a 5 b $-\left(-\dfrac{1}{5}\right)$ c 0 d None of these

11. The value of $m+n$ that satisfies the given expression $(3^{30}+3^{-30})(3^{30}-3^{-30})=3^m-3^{-n}$ is

   a 30 b 60 c 120 d 90

12. Four students distributed posters around their school. The table shows the fraction of the total number of posters each student distributed:

	Students		Fraction of posters distributed
A.	Ajay	i.	$\dfrac{3}{10}$
B.	Ramu	ii.	$\dfrac{1}{4}$
C.	Sonu	iii.	$\dfrac{1}{20}$
D.	Tony	iv.	$\dfrac{2}{5}$

Tell which student has distributed the greatest number of posters and difference between the smallest and greatest?

   a Ajay, $\dfrac{2}{20}$ b Ramu, $\dfrac{6}{20}$ c Sonu, $\dfrac{1}{20}$ d Tony, $\dfrac{7}{20}$

13. A sum of money put out at compound interest amounts in two years to ₹ 578.40 and in three years to ₹ 614.55. Then, the rate of interest is

   a 6% b $6\dfrac{1}{4}\%$ c $6\dfrac{1}{2}$ d $6\dfrac{3}{4}\%$

14. If 4 women or 3 men earn ₹ 960 in one day. Then, earning of 12 women and 7 men in 5 days will be

   a ₹ 2560   b ₹ 25600   c ₹ 9600   d ₹ 2500

15. The value of the expression $\dfrac{4}{25} \times \dfrac{2}{5} - \dfrac{64}{25}$ is

   a $\dfrac{8}{25}$ b $\left(\dfrac{2}{5}\right)^3 \times \left(-\dfrac{3}{5}\right)$

   c $\dfrac{2^3}{5^3}$ d None of these

16. If $\sqrt{0.09 \times 0.9 \times a} = 0.009 \times 0.9 \times \sqrt{b}$, then $\dfrac{a}{b}$ is

   a 81×10^{-5} b 81×10^{-2}

   c 9×10^{-4} d 9×10^{-2}

17. If the difference between a number and its reciprocal is 5. Then, the difference between their cubes will be

   a 140   b 110   c 125   d 90

18. Two years ago, Sahil was three times as old as his son and two years hence, twice his age will be equal to five times that of his son. Then, present age of Sahil and his son are respectively

   a 38 yr and 16 yr   b 28 yr and 14 yr

   c 38 yr and 14 yr   d 35 yr and 14 yr

19. If $(a + b) : (b + c) : (c + a) = 6 : 7 : 8$ and sum of the numbers a, b, c is 14. Then, the value of c is

   a 6   b 8   c 14   d 7

20. If the angle bisector of given parallelogram $UVWX$ intersect each other at $ABCD$, then the measure of $\angle A$ is

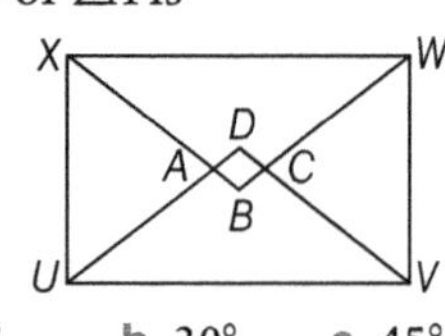

   a 60°   b 30°   c 45°   d 90°

21. The least number by which 294 must be multiplied to make it a perfect square, is

   a 2   b 3   c 6   d 12

22. For what value of y, the value of equation

$$y^2 + 2y - 3 = 0, \text{ if } \left(\dfrac{5}{2}\right)^{-4} \times \left(\dfrac{5}{2}\right)^{-5} = \left(\dfrac{5}{2}\right)^{3y}?$$

   a 3   b −3   c 9   d 4

23. Three angles of a triangle are in the ratio $1 : 2 : 3$. The sum of the smallest and greatest angles is

   a 90°   b 100°   c 120°   d 150°

24. At the rate of 8% per annum. If the compound interest is more than simple interest by ₹ 160 for two years. Then, the amount deposited would be

   a ₹ 30000   b ₹ 25000

   c ₹ 24000   d ₹ 20000

25. If $ABCD$ is a square and CDE is an equilateral triangle, then the value of $\angle AEB$ is

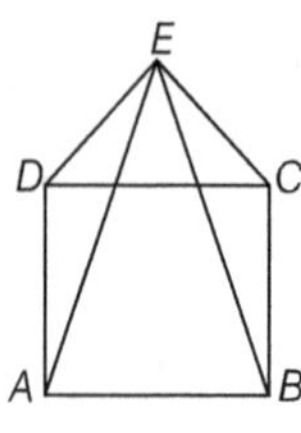

   a 15°   b 20°   c 25°   d 30°

26. Sum of additive inverse of $\dfrac{4}{5} \times \left(-\dfrac{2}{5}\right)$ and reciprocal of $\left(-\dfrac{10}{8}\right) \times \left(\dfrac{25}{8}\right)$ is

   a $\dfrac{25}{64}$ b $\dfrac{72}{125}$

   c $\dfrac{8}{25}$ d None of these

27. A number x is such that $5^{2x+1} \div 25 = 125$. Then, the value of x is

   a 1   b 2   c 3   d 0

28. The area of a rectangular field is in the form of $x^2 - 4x - 12$. If the length of wire of fencing around the field is 24 cm. Then, the value of x is

   a 10   b 8   c 12   d 16

29. If the cost of 20 greeting cards is equal to the selling price of 16 greeting cards. Then, the gain or loss per cent is

   a 20%   b 25%   c 30%   d 40%

30. In the given figure, if $AB \parallel DC$ and $AD = BC$ and height is 8 cm. Then, the value of x is

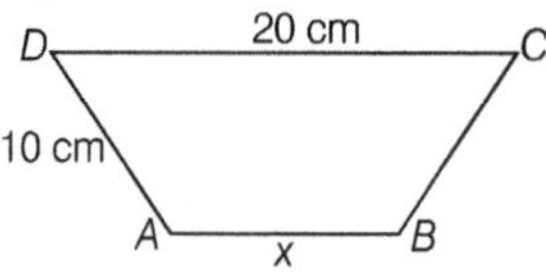

   a 8 cm   b 20 cm   c 5 cm   d 15 cm

Answers

1. *b*	2. *c*	3. *b*	4. *b*	5. *c*	6. *b*	7. *b*	8. *b*	9. *a*	10. *b*
11. *c*	12. *d*	13. *b*	14. *b*	15. *d*	16. *a*	17. *a*	18. *c*	19. *a*	20. *d*
21. *c*	22. *b*	23. *c*	24. *b*	25. *d*	26. *d*	27. *b*	28. *b*	29. *b*	30. *a*

MATHEMATICS OLYMPIAD CLASS VIII

Practice Set 3

Practice Set 4

A Whole Content Based Test for Class 8th Mathematics Olympiad

1. Which of the following statements is necessarily true about division of the two rational numbers?
   a Division of two rational numbers is closed under rational numbers.
   b Division of two rational numbers is commutative.
   c Both (a) and (b).
   d None of the above.

2. After solving the expression $(3^{-4} + 4^{-3} + 5^{-1} + 6^{-2} + 7^{-1})^0$, we will get
   a 22   b −1   c 1   d 0

3. Which step is wrong in the given factorisation of a polynomial?

   Step I $x^2 - 6x + 8$

   Step II $x^2 - 4x - 2x + 8$

   Step III $x(x - 4) - 2(x - 4)$

   Step IV $(x - 2)(x - 4)$

   a Step I   b Step II
   c Step III   d No step is wrong.

4. There are … numbers of rational numbers between the rational numbers $\dfrac{2}{3}$ and $\dfrac{8}{3}$.

   a 5   b 7
   c infinite   d None of these

5. If A, B, C and D are four quantities such that $A:B = 3:4$, $B:C = 8:9$, $C:D = 15:16$. Then, $A:D$ is
   a 5 : 8   b 8 : 5
   c 4 : 5   d 5 : 4

6. The value of x, if $6:8 :: x:15$, is

   a 20   b $\dfrac{45}{4}$

   c $\dfrac{26}{5}$ d None of these

7. The age of a man is same as his wife's age with the digits reversed. Then, sum of their ages is 99 yr and the man is 9 yr older than his wife. Man's age is
   a 52 yr   b 49 yr   c 44 yr   d 54 yr

8. $\boxed{10^x} \times \boxed{(2 \times 5)^y} \times \boxed{\left(\dfrac{20}{2}\right)^z} \times \boxed{\left(\dfrac{40}{4}\right)^r} = \boxed{[2 \times (25)^{1/2}]^{12}}$

   The average value of x, y, z and r will be
   a 3   b 4   c 2   d 5

9. Multiplicative inverse of product of additive inverse of −5/2 and reciprocal of −1 is
   a 0   b 1   c $\dfrac{5}{2}$ d $\dfrac{-2}{5}$

10. Which method is used in steps of factorisation shown below?
    Step I $x^2 - 49$
    Step II $(x)^2 - (7)^2$
    Step III $(x - 7)(x + 7)$
    Step IV Factors are $(x - 7)$ and $(x + 7)$.
    a Identity
    b Middle term factorisation
    c Rearrangement
    d Completing square

11. Simple interest on an amount for two years at the rate of 6% per annum is ₹ 300. Then, the compound interest on the same amount for the same time period and same rate of interest will be
    a ₹ 310   b ₹ 308   c ₹ 307   d ₹ 309

12. A motorboat covers a certain distance downstream in a river in 5 h. It covers the same distance upstream in $5\dfrac{1}{2}$ h. The speed of the water is 1.5 km/h. Then, the speed of the boat in still water is
    a 30 km/h   b 30.5 km/h
    c 20 km/h   d 31.5 km/h

13. As we know that, weight and length of a rod is directly proportion. If 6 m long rod can weight 30 kg and 7 m long rod can weight 35 kg. Then, how much weight a 25 m long rod can have?
    a 105 kg   b 250 kg   c 125 kg   d 140 kg

14. Two matchsticks each of length 7 cm are crossing each other such that they bisect each other at right angles. What shape will be formed by joining their end points?
    a Rectangle   b Square
    c Rhombus   d Parallelogram

15. The additive inverse of $\dfrac{4}{11} \times \left(\dfrac{2}{5} - \dfrac{4}{10} \right)$ is

    a not possible   **b** 0

    c 1   **d** None of these

16. The sum of two numbers is 15 and the difference of their squares is 45. Then, the difference of the numbers is

    a 4   **b** 3   **c** 0   **d** 1

17. If the difference between the simple and compound interest compounded every six months at the rate of 10% per annum at the end of two years is ₹ 124.05. Then, the amount (principal) will be

    a ₹ 10000   **b** ₹ 6000

    c ₹ 12000   **d** ₹ 8000

18. If a man walking at the speed of 4 km/h crosses a square field diagonally in 3 min. Then, how much time it will take to cross the field by side?

    a 6 min   **b** 4.23 min

    c 5 min   **d** 8 min

19. The simplified value of the expression $\dfrac{3 \cdot 2^{n+1} + 2^{n-1}}{2^{n+2} - \left(\dfrac{1}{2} \right)^{1-n}}$ is equal to, if $n = 2$

    a 2   **b** $\dfrac{1}{2}$ **c** $\dfrac{13}{7}$ **d** $\dfrac{52}{15}$

20. Nisha thinks a number and subtracts $\dfrac{5}{2}$ from it. She multiplies the result by 8, the result now obtained is 3 times the same number, she thought of. What is the number?

    a 5   **b** 14

    c 4   **d** None of these

21. Two pipes A and B can fill a tank in 30 min and 45 min, respectively. A is opened initially and when it is half filled B is also opened. How much time, it will take to fill the tank completely?

    a 35 min   **b** 24 min

    c 25 min   **d** 40 min

22. If $\dfrac{1}{5} : \dfrac{1}{x} = \dfrac{1}{x} : \dfrac{1}{125}$, then the value of x is

    a 20   **b** 5   **c** 25   **d** 125

23. In adjoining figure, ABC is a right angled triangle and O is the mid point of the side opposite to the right angle. Then, the value of OB and OC, if $OA = 5$ cm, is

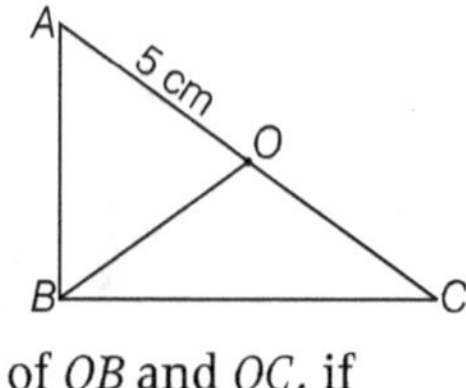

    a 10 cm each   **b** 8 cm and 5 cm

    c 5 cm each   **d** 2.5 cm each

24. The area of a circle is given by the expression $\pi x^2 + 6\pi x + 9\pi$. If the radius of the circle is a perfect square number. Then, the least possible value of x to be found is

    a 6   **b** 3   **c** 1   **d** 13

25. Megha buys $\dfrac{39}{83}$ kg ghee at the rate of ₹ 166 per kg, $\dfrac{3}{5}$ kg butter at the rate of ₹ 90 per kg and $\dfrac{9}{5}$ kg peas at the rate of ₹ 75 per kg. If she gives a ₹ 1000 note to the shopkeeper, how much change should she get back?

    a 267   **b** 265   **c** 733   **d** 775

26. By what least number should 33075 be multiplied to obtain a perfect cube?

    a 15   **b** 21   **c** 35   **d** 30

27. A man plants 23716 mango trees in his garden and arranges them so that there are as many rows as there are mangoes tree in each row. The number of rows is

    a 146   **b** 156   **c** 154   **d** 164

28. P is twice as fast as Q and Q is thrice as fast as R. If P covers a distance in 21 min, then in how many minutes will K cover the distance?

    a 7   **b** 14   **c** 49   **d** 126

29. If the value of $(7 + 3x)$ is equal to $(7 - 3x)$, then the value of $(7x^2 + 4x + 9)$ is equal to

    a 11   **b** 9   **c** 20   **d** 3

30. If $\dfrac{m}{n} = \dfrac{o}{p} = \dfrac{q}{r}$, then the value of $\dfrac{m^2 + o^2 + q^2 + mo + oq + mq}{n^2 + p^2 + r^2 + np + pr + nr}$ is

    a 0   **b** 1   **c** $\dfrac{m + o + q}{n + p + r}$ **d** $\dfrac{moq}{npr}$

Answers

1. *a*	2. *c*	3. *d*	4. *c*	5. *a*	6. *b*	7. *d*	8. *a*	9. *d*	10. *a*
11. *d*	12. *d*	13. *c*	14. *b*	15. *b*	16. *b*	17. *c*	18. *b*	19. *c*	20. *c*
21. *b*	22. *c*	23. *c*	24. *c*	25. *c*	26. *c*	27. *c*	28. *d*	29. *b*	30. *b*

Practice Set 4

Practice Set 5

A Whole Content Based Test for Class 8th Mathematics Olympiad

1. Simplify $\sqrt[3]{\sqrt{0.015625}}$.
   - a 0.05
   - b 0.5
   - c 5
   - d None of these

2. What is the unit digit in the product $(4537)^{153} \times (251)^{72}$?
   - a 1
   - b 3
   - c 5
   - d 7

3. The sum of two numbers is 11. Five times one number is equal to 6 times the other. The bigger of the two numbers is
   - a 5
   - b 6
   - c 8
   - d 9

4. Father's age is three times more than his son Pranit. After 8 yr, he would be two and a half times of Pranit's age. After further 8 yr, how many times would he be Pranit's age?
   - a 2 times
   - b $2\frac{1}{2}$ times
   - c $2\frac{3}{4}$ times
   - d 3 times

5. 4% of income of P is equal to 12% of income of Q and 8% of income of Q is equal to 16% of income of R. If R's income is ₹ 2000, then the total income of P, Q and R is
   - a ₹ 6000
   - b ₹ 14000
   - c ₹ 18000
   - d ₹ 20000

6. Pure ghee costs ₹ 90 per kg. After adulterating it with vegetable oil costing ₹ 45 per kg, a shopkeeper sells the mixture at the rate of ₹ 84 thereby making a profit of 20%. In what ratio does he mix the two?
   - a 3 : 2
   - b 5 : 4
   - c 6 : 7
   - d 2 : 1

7. Mehak works 4 h a day to edit 15 pages having 10 questions on each page. If she has to edit 20 pages having 15 questions in a day, how many hours she needs to work?
   - a 4
   - b 8
   - c 10
   - d None of these

8. A certain amount becomes ₹ 952 in 3 yr at a certain rate of simple interest. If the rate of interest is increased by 25%, what amount will ₹ 800 become in 3 yr?
   - a ₹ 1008
   - b ₹ 1160
   - c ₹ 1052
   - d None of these

9.

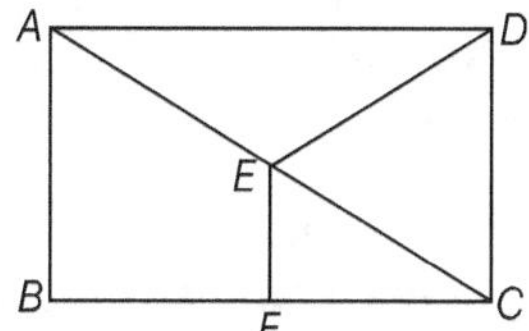

In the above figure, $ABCD$ is a rectangle with $DE \perp AC$ and $EF \perp BC$. If $\angle FEC$ is 42°, then $\angle EDC$ and $\angle BAC$ are respectively
   - a 48° and 42°
   - b 42° and 48°
   - c 54° and 36
   - d 36° and 54°

10. The third proportional to $(a^2 - b^2)$ and $(a - b)$ is
   - a $a + b$
   - b $a - b$
   - c $\dfrac{a + b}{a - b}$
   - d $\dfrac{a - b}{a + b}$

11. The polynomial $8x^3 + y^3 + 27z^3 - 18xyz$ on factorisation gives
   - a $(2x + y + 3z)(4x^2 + y^2 + 9z^2 + 2xy + 3yz + 6xz)$
   - b $(2x + y + 3z)^2$
   - c $(2x + y + 3z)(4x^2 + y^2 + 9z^2 - 2xy - 3yz - 6xz)$
   - d $(2x + y + 3z)(4x^2 + y^2 + 9z^2 - 4xy - 6yz - 12xz)$

12. If $xyz = 8$ and $x + y + z = 8$, then $\dfrac{1}{xy} + \dfrac{1}{yz} + \dfrac{1}{xz}$ is equal to
   - a 0
   - b 1
   - c 8
   - d 64

13. In a test, Minakshi got 30% of the maximum marks and failed by 10 marks. Whereas, Sonam got 40% of the maximum marks and got 20 marks more than the passing marks. What are the passing marks?

   a 40   b 90
   c 100   d 120

14. Ravi had to arrange 9604 flowers in rows such that the number of rows is equal to the number of flowers in each row, find how many rows must be formed?

   a 78   b 92
   c 98   d 88

15. Ragini sold two articles. She sold one of them at 20% profit for ₹ 180 and the other at 25% loss at ₹ 150. Find her overall profit/loss percentage approximately.

   a 5.7% loss   b 8.8% profit
   c 5.9% loss   d 7.2% profit

16. If a sum becomes A in 1 yr at the rate of 6% compounded annually, then find out in how many years it will become $1.06A$ of A at the same rate?

   a 2 yr   b 3 yr
   c 1.5 yr   d 3.5 yr

17. The value of $\dfrac{(53.642)^2 - (46.358)^2}{(74.249) - (66.965)}$ is

   a 1.04   b 10.8
   c 100   d 40

18. If two trains running at different speeds (where, a, b such that $a > b$) reach each other in r h while running in same direction and in q h while running from opposite directions, distance being same. Then, what is the relation between the speeds of the trains?

   a $\dfrac{r+q}{r-q}$ b $\dfrac{r-q}{r+q}$
   c $\dfrac{a+r}{b+q}$ d 1

19. In factory A, the ratio of married workers to unmarried workers is $5 : 4$. In factory B, the ratio of married workers to unmarried workers is $2 : 7$. After 10 unmarried workers leave factory A to join factory B, the ratio of married workers to unmarried workers in factory B becomes $4 : 15$. How many unmarried workers are there in factory B now?

   a 130   b 135
   c 150   d 160

20. Monika stiches 7 clothes working 4 h a day in 9 days. If she needs to complete the stiching in 6 days, how many hours does she need to work in a day?

   a 7 h   b 6 h
   c 8 h   d 12 h

21. The difference between the simple interest received from two different banks on ₹ 4000 for 2 yr is ₹ 60, the difference between their rates of interest is

   a 0.25%   b 0.50%
   c 0.75%   d 1%

22. The compound interest on ₹ 60000 for 3 yr, compounded annually and the rate of interest being 10%, 12% and 15% for the three successive years respectively, will be

   a ₹ 25468   b ₹ 25008
   c ₹ 25018   d ₹ 25088

23. 5 men or 15 women can complete a job in 30 days. In how many days can 3 men and 5 women complete it?

   a 20 days
   b 28 days
   c 40 days
   d None of the above

24. A square $ABCD$ of side 8 cm is shown below with $\triangle PQB$ having all sides equal to 6 cm. Find the side RB.

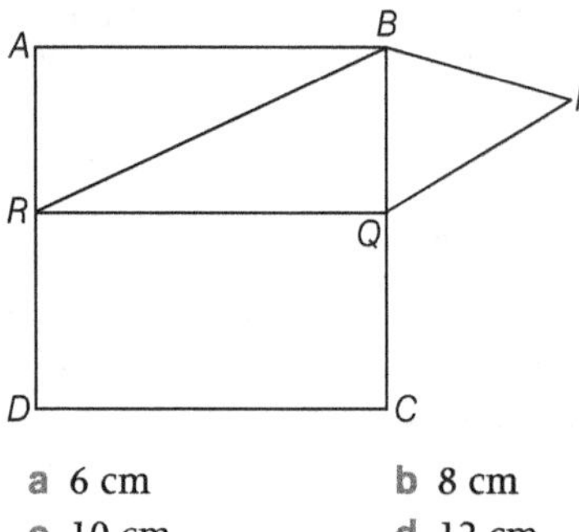

   a 6 cm   b 8 cm
   c 10 cm   d 12 cm

25. Jerry cut-out a piece of cake in such a way that it was four-sided and had exactly two distinct consecutive pairs of sides of equal length. Which shape is cut-out by him?

   a Square
   b Rectangle
   c Kite
   d Rhombus

26. Renuka bought two chairs for ₹ 1200 each. She sold one at a profit of 5% and the other at a loss of 10%. What is the selling price of each chair, if both are sold at a profit of 15%. Find the difference between the new profit and the previous profit/loss, whatever it may be.

    a ₹ 1380, ₹ 360
    b ₹ 2760, ₹ 420
    c ₹ 1380, ₹ 420
    d ₹ 2760, ₹ 360

27. Consider the given below figure:

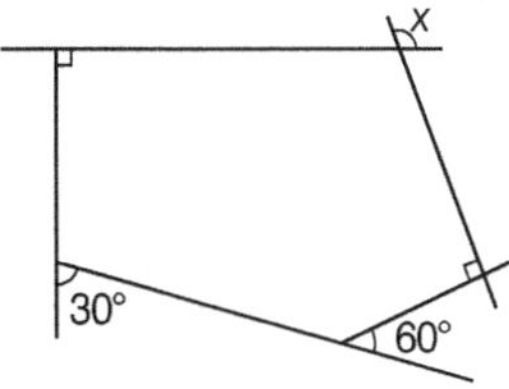

Find the value of x.

    a 60°
    b 90°
    c 120°
    d 150°

28. Find the value of

$$\left\{ \left[\left(\frac{1}{4}\right)^{-1} - \left(\frac{1}{5}\right)^{-1} \right] + \left[\left(\frac{1}{7}\right)^{-1} - \left(\frac{1}{8}\right)^{-1} \right] + \left[\left(\frac{1}{3}\right)^{-1} - \left(\frac{1}{2}\right)^{-1} \right] \right\}^{4}$$

    a 2   b 3   c 1   d −1

29. Find the missing digit y in $1040y$, so that the number is a perfect square.

    a 1   b 3   c 4   d 7

30. What is the speed of the boat in still water?

    I. It takes 2 h to cover the distance between A and B downstream.

    II. It takes 4 h to cover the distance between A and B upstream.

    Give answer

    a if the data in Statement I alone is sufficient
    b if the data in Statement II alone is sufficient
    c if the data in both Statements I and II are required to answer
    d if the data even in both Statements I and II together are not sufficient

Answers

1. *b*	2. *d*	3. *b*	4. *a*	5. *c*	6. *b*	7. *b*	8. *b*	9. *a*	10. *d*
11. *c*	12. *b*	13. *c*	14. *c*	15. *a*	16. *a*	17. *c*	18. *a*	19. *c*	20. *b*
21. *c*	22. *b*	23. *b*	24. *c*	25. *c*	26. *c*	27. *b*	28. *c*	29. *c*	30. *d*

Answer & Explanations

① Rational Number

1. *d*	2. *c*	3. *c*	4. *c*	5. *c*	6. *b*	7. *c*	8. *c*	9. *b*	10. *b*
11. *c*	12. *b*	13. *b*	14. *b*	15. *d*	16. *a*	17. *b*	18. *b*	19. *b*	20. *c*
21. *b*	22. *b*	23. *b*	24. *b*	25. *a*	26. *b*				

② Exponent and Power

1. *b*	2. *b*	3. *a*	4. *a*	5. *b*	6. *c*	7. *b*	8. *a*	9. *b*	10. *d*
11. *d*	12. *c*	13. *b*	14. *a*	15. *c*	16. *b*	17. *d*	18. *a*	19. *a*	20. *a*
21. *c*	22. *c*	23. *b*	24. *c*	25. *c*	26. *a*				

③ Square and Square Root

1. *c*	2. *d*	3. *d*	4. *b*	5. *d*	6. *c*	7. *c*	8. *a*	9. *d*	10. *c*
11. *a*	12. *c*	13. *b*	14. *a*	15. *b*	16. *a*	17. *a*	18. *d*	19. *c*	20. *d*
21. *c*	22. *b*	23. *a*	24. *a*						

④ Cube and Cube Root

1. *a*	2. *d*	3. *b*	4. *b*	5. *b*	6. *c*	7. *b*	8. *a*	9. *b*	10. *c*
11. *a*	12. *b*	13. *c*	14. *c*	15. *b*	16. *b*	17. *c*	18. *d*	19. *c*	20. *c*
21. *a*	22. *a*								

⑤ Algebraic Expressions

1. *c*	2. *c*	3. *b*	4. *c*	5. *c*	6. *d*	7. *a*	8. *a*	9. *b*	10. *a*
11. *b*	12. *b*	13. *b*	14. *b*	15. *b*	16. *a*	17. *b*	18. *a*	19. *c*	20. *b*
21. *d*	22. *c*	23. *c*	24. *b*	25. *a*	26. *a*	27. *a*	28. *b*		

⑥ Factorisation of Algebraic Expressions

1. *d*	2. *a*	3. *b*	4. *b*	5. *a*	6. *c*	7. *c*	8. *b*	9. *c*	10. *b*
11. *c*	12. *d*	13. *c*	14. *c*	15. *c*	16. *a*	17. *a*	18. *c*	19. *a*	20. *a*

⑦ Linear Equation in One Variable

1. *a*	2. *c*	3. *a*	4. *c*	5. *b*	6. *a*	7. *d*	8. *a*	9. *c*	10. *b*
11. *b*	12. *b*	13. *b*	14. *a*	15. *a*	16. *c*	17. *b*	18. *b*	19. *d*	20. *c*
21. *a*	22. *c*	23. *c*	24. *a*						

⑧ Profit, Loss and Discount

1. *c*	2. *a*	3. *b*	4. *d*	5. *c*	6. *c*	7. *c*	8. *c*	9. *b*	10. *b*
11. *b*	12. *a*	13. *b*	14. *a*	15. *c*	16. *b*	17. *a*	18. *a*		

MATHEMATICS OLYMPIAD CLASS VIII

⑨ Simple and Compound Interest

1. *a*	2. *c*	3. *b*	4. *a*	5. *b*	6. *a*	7. *b*	8. *a*	9. *a*	10. *c*
11. *c*	12. *b*	13. *c*	14. *a*	15. *a*	16. *b*	17. *a*	18. *a*		

⑩ Direct and Inverse Proportion

1. *b*	2. *b*	3. *c*	4. *c*	5. *c*	6. *b*	7. *a*	8. *c*	9. *c*	10. *b*
11. *b*	12. *b*	13. *a*	14. *c*	15. *b*	16. *a*	17. *b*	18. *b*	19. *b*	20. *b*
21. *b*	22. *b*	23. *b*	24. *c*	25. *b*	26. *d*	27. *b*	28. *a*	29. *c*	30. *a*
31. *a*									

⑪ Quadrilaterals

1. *a*	2. *a*	3. *c*	4. *d*	5. *b*	6. *b*	7. *b*	8. *a*	9. *b*	10. *c*
11. *a*	12. *b*	13. *a*	14. *b*	15. *b*	16. *c*	17. *a*	18. *a*		

<h1>① Rational Number</h1>

2. $\dfrac{2}{5} + \dfrac{15}{25} - 5 + \dfrac{7}{15}$

$= \dfrac{2}{5} + \dfrac{3}{5} - 5 + \dfrac{7}{15}$

$= \dfrac{5}{5} - 5 + \dfrac{7}{15}$

$= \dfrac{5-25}{5} + \dfrac{7}{15} = \dfrac{-20}{5} + \dfrac{7}{15}$

$= \dfrac{-60+7}{15} = -\dfrac{53}{15}$

4. $\dfrac{81}{27} = 3$ [a natural number]

6. Sum of two rational numbers $= -3$

One of them $= \dfrac{-6}{7}$ [given]

Then,   other number $= -3 - \left(-\dfrac{6}{7}\right)$

$= \dfrac{6}{7} - 3 = \dfrac{6-21}{7}$

$= -\dfrac{15}{7}$

7. According to the question,

$\left(\dfrac{77}{14} + \dfrac{195}{26}\right) \div \left(\dfrac{77}{14} - \dfrac{195}{26}\right)$

We have, $\dfrac{77}{14} = \dfrac{11}{2}$

and $\dfrac{195}{26} = \dfrac{15}{2}$

$\therefore$ $\left(\dfrac{11}{2} + \dfrac{15}{2}\right) \div \left(\dfrac{11}{2} - \dfrac{15}{2}\right)$

$= \left(\dfrac{26}{2}\right) \div \left(\dfrac{-4}{2}\right)$

$= 13 \div (-2)$

$= -\dfrac{13}{2}$

Or

$\left(\dfrac{11}{2} + \dfrac{15}{2}\right) \div \left(\dfrac{15}{2} - \dfrac{11}{2}\right)$

[we take difference, greater – smaller, when not defined]

$= 13 \div 2 = \dfrac{13}{2} = \dfrac{91}{14}$

[according to the option]

8. Given, $a = \dfrac{1}{5}$

Consider, $-\left(-\dfrac{a-1}{a}\right)$

$= -\left(-1 + \dfrac{1}{a}\right)$

$= -(5 - 1)$

$= -4 = -\dfrac{1}{\frac{1}{4}}$

10. $4 + \dfrac{1}{m + \dfrac{1}{n}} = \dfrac{56}{12}$ [given]

$\Rightarrow$ $4 + \dfrac{1}{m + \dfrac{1}{n}} = 4 + \dfrac{8}{12}$

$\left[\because \dfrac{56}{12} - 4 = \dfrac{8}{12}\right]$

$\Rightarrow$ $m + \dfrac{1}{n} = \dfrac{12}{8}$ [by comparing]

$\Rightarrow$ $m + \dfrac{1}{n} = 1 + \dfrac{4}{8}$

$\Rightarrow$ $m + \dfrac{1}{n} = 1 + \dfrac{1}{2}$

$\Rightarrow$ $m = 1, n = 2$ [by comparing]

$\therefore$ $m + n = 1 + 2 = 3$

11. $(C + E) - (A + B) \div (G - H)$

$= \left(0 + \dfrac{9}{11}\right) - \left(-\dfrac{9}{7} - \dfrac{8}{7}\right) \div \left(\dfrac{14}{6} - \dfrac{15}{6}\right)$

$= \dfrac{9}{11} + \dfrac{17}{7} \div \left(-\dfrac{1}{6}\right)$

$= \dfrac{9}{11} - \dfrac{17}{7} \times 6$

$= \dfrac{63 - 1122}{77} = -\dfrac{1059}{77}$

13. Let the numbers be x and y.

Then, $x + y = 12$

and $xy = 35$

$\therefore$ $\dfrac{x+y}{xy} = \dfrac{12}{35}$

$\Rightarrow$ $\dfrac{1}{y} + \dfrac{1}{x} = \dfrac{12}{35}$

14. In A, B and D, the distributive properties are used, while in case of C, the property is wrongly used.   [invalid]

16.   I. False   II. True

     III. False   IV. True

     V. True

17.   I. $-(-x) \div x^{-1} \times x + x$

$= x \div \dfrac{1}{x} \times x + x$

$= x^2 \times x + x$

$= x^3 + x$

$= (x^2 + 1)\, x$

   II. $\left(\dfrac{3}{2} - \dfrac{2}{3}\right) - (-\square) = -\dfrac{1}{6}$

$\Rightarrow$ $(-\square) = \dfrac{3}{2} - \dfrac{2}{3} + \dfrac{1}{6}$

$\Rightarrow$ $(-\square) = \dfrac{9 - 4 + 1}{6}$

$= \dfrac{6}{6} = 1$

$\therefore$ $\square = -1$

III. Given, $m * n = \dfrac{m}{n} - \dfrac{n}{m}$

$\therefore$ $9 * 18 = \dfrac{9}{18} - \dfrac{18}{9}$

$= \dfrac{1}{2} - 2 = -\dfrac{3}{2}$

IV. $\dfrac{\dfrac{1}{4} + \dfrac{3}{2}}{\dfrac{1}{4} - \dfrac{3}{2}} = \dfrac{\dfrac{1+6}{4}}{\dfrac{1-6}{4}}$

$= \dfrac{\dfrac{7}{4}}{-\dfrac{5}{4}} = -\dfrac{7}{5}$

18. Given, $3254p06q$ to be exactly divisible by 3 and 5,

then q should be either 0 or 5 to be divisible by 5.

Now, sum of numbers $= 20 + p + q$

Now, $20 + p + q$ to be divisible by 3 should be a multiple of 3.

From the given options, $p + q$ should be equal to 13 such that $20 + 13 = 33$ is divisible by 3.

19. Length of cloth needed for 16 shirts $= 24$ m   [given]

$\therefore$ Length of cloth needed for 1 shirt

$= \dfrac{24}{16}\text{m} = \dfrac{3}{2}$ m

$\therefore$ Length of cloth needed for 12 shirts

$= 12 \times \dfrac{3}{2} = 18$ m

20. Let total number of students be 100.

Number of students come to school by car $= 100 \times \dfrac{2}{5} = 40$

Remaining $= 100 - 40 = 60$

Number of students come to school by bus $= 60 \times \dfrac{1}{4} = 15$

$\therefore$ Rest students $= 100 - (40 + 15)$

$= 45$

If 45 students come by walking, then total number of students $= 100$

If 180 come by walking, then total number of students

$= \dfrac{100 \times 180}{45} = 400$

21. According to the question,

$\dfrac{3}{5} - \dfrac{2}{7} = \dfrac{21 - 10}{35} = \dfrac{11}{35}$

Since, $\dfrac{11}{35}$ equivalents to 44.

Now, 1 equivalents to

$\dfrac{44 \times 35}{11}$ i.e. 140.

$\therefore$ Sum of digits of number $= 1 + 4 + 0 = 5$

MATHEMATICS OLYMPIAD CLASS VIII

22. Total income of Raju = ₹ 12000   [given]

$\therefore$ Expenditure on food

$$= ₹\, 12000 \times \frac{1}{4} = ₹\, 3000$$

Remaining money

$$= ₹\, (12000 - 3000) = ₹\, 9000$$

Expenditure on house rent

$$= ₹\, 9000 \times \frac{3}{10} = ₹\, 2700$$

Remaining amount after rent

$$= ₹\, (9000 - 2700) = ₹\, 6300$$

Expenditure on education

$$= ₹\, 6300 \times \frac{5}{21} = ₹\, 1500$$

$\therefore$ Money saved (or left after expenditure on education)

$$= ₹\, (6300 - 1500) = ₹\, 4800$$

23. Cost of 5 hot dogs = ₹ 60

$\therefore$ Cost of 3 hot dogs $= \dfrac{60}{5} \times 3 = ₹\, 36$

Cost of 4 pastries = ₹ 20

$\therefore$ Cost of 2 pastries $= \dfrac{20}{4} \times 2 = ₹\, 10$

Cost of 3 rolls = ₹ 60

$\therefore$ Cost of 4 rolls $= \dfrac{60}{3} \times 4 = ₹\, 80$

$\therefore$ Total cost $= ₹\,(36 + 10 + 80)$
$$= ₹\, 126$$

Total money Raju have = ₹ 200

$\therefore$ Money left $= ₹\,(200 - 126) = ₹\, 74$

$\therefore$ Required rational number,

$$\frac{p}{q} = \frac{74}{200}$$

24. Improvement made by Ajay

$$= \frac{35}{60} - \frac{30}{60} = \frac{5}{60}$$

Improvement made by Sonu

$$= \frac{50}{60} - \frac{42}{70} = \frac{98}{420} = \frac{7}{30}$$

Improvement made by Manish

$$= \frac{42}{50} - \frac{50}{60} = \frac{252 - 250}{300}$$

$$= \frac{2}{300} = \frac{1}{150}$$

We see that, $\dfrac{7}{30} > \dfrac{5}{60} > \dfrac{1}{150}$

Hence, Sonu made the most improvement.

25. Sugar required in first recipe

$$= \frac{2}{5} \text{ cup of sugar}$$

Sugar required in second recipe
= 5 tablespoons of sugar

$$= 5 \times \frac{1}{15} = \frac{1}{3} \text{ cup of sugar}$$

$\therefore$ More sugar needed by Ist recipe

$$= \frac{2}{5} - \frac{1}{3} = \frac{6 - 5}{15} = \frac{1}{15} \text{ cup}$$

$$= 1 \text{ tablespoon}$$

26. Total allowance for each of them
$$= ₹1260$$

In case of Sohan,

Money left $= ₹\, 84 = \dfrac{84}{1260} = \dfrac{1}{15}$

Since, both Mohan and Sohan are left with equal amount.

$\therefore$ Money spent at mall by Mohan

$$= \left(1 - \frac{1}{15}\right) - \frac{1}{2}$$

$$= \frac{14}{15} - \frac{1}{2}$$

$$= \frac{28 - 15}{30} = \frac{13}{30}$$

② *Exponent and Power*

1. $(a^m \cdot a^n) \div \dfrac{a^m}{a^n} = a^{m+n} \div a^{m-n}$

$$= a^{m+n-m+n} = a^{2n}$$

Here, $a = 2 \Rightarrow 2^{2n}$

2. $(x^4)^{-3} = x^{4 \times (-3)} = x^{-12}$

$$[\because (x^a)^b = (x^b)^a = x^{ab}]$$

3. $\dfrac{(-2)^x \times (-2)^7}{3 \times 4^6} = \dfrac{1}{12}$ [given]

$\Rightarrow \qquad \dfrac{(-2)^{x+7}}{3 \times (2^2)^6} = \dfrac{1}{12}$

$\Rightarrow \qquad \dfrac{(-2)^{x+7}}{3 \times 2^{12}} = \dfrac{1}{12}$

$\Rightarrow \qquad \dfrac{(-2)^{x+7-12}}{3} = \dfrac{1}{12}$

$\Rightarrow \qquad (-2)^{x-5} = \dfrac{1}{4}$

$\Rightarrow \qquad (-2)^{x-5} = (-2)^{-2}$

$$[\because (-2)^n = 2^n, \text{ when } n \in \text{even}]$$

$\Rightarrow \quad x - 5 = -2$ [by comparing]

$\therefore \qquad x = 3$

4. $-(-2)^3 - (-3)^2 + (-3)^4$

$$= -(-8) - (9) + 81$$
$$= 8 - 9 + 81$$
$$= 80$$

5. $[1^{-2} + 2^{-2} + 3^{-2}] \times 6^2$

$$= \left[1 + \frac{1}{4} + \frac{1}{9}\right] \times 36$$

$$= \frac{36 + 9 + 4}{36} \times 36 = 49$$

6. $\dfrac{5^m \times 5^3 \times 5^{-2}}{5^{-3} \times 5^{-2}} = 5^{12}$

$\Rightarrow \qquad \dfrac{5^{m+3-2}}{5^{-3-2}} = 5^{12}$

$\Rightarrow \qquad 5^{m+1+5} = 5^{12}$

$\Rightarrow \qquad 5^{m+6} = 5^{12}$

$\therefore \quad m + 6 = 12$ [by comparing]

$\Rightarrow \quad m = 6$

7. $2^x + 2^x + 2^x = 192$

$\Rightarrow \qquad 3 \times 2^x = 192$

$\Rightarrow \qquad 2^x = 64 = 2^6$

$\therefore \qquad x = 6$ [by comparing]

8. $\dfrac{(16)^{2m+1} \cdot (64)^5}{(256)^2 \cdot 4} = (256)^{3m}$

$\Rightarrow \quad \dfrac{16^{2m+1} \cdot 64^5}{4} = (256)^{3m+2}$

$\Rightarrow \quad \dfrac{16^{2m+1} \cdot 16^5 \cdot 4^5}{4} = (256)^{3m+2}$

$\Rightarrow \quad 16^{2m+6} \cdot 4^4 = (256)^{3m+2}$

$\Rightarrow \quad 16^{2m+6} = (256)^{3m+1}$

$$[\because 4^4 = 256]$$

$\Rightarrow \quad (16)^{2m+6} = \{(16)^2\}^{3m+1}$

$\Rightarrow \quad 2m + 6 = 6m + 2$

               [by comparing]

$\Rightarrow \qquad 4m = 4$

$\therefore \qquad m = 1$

9. $(36)^{1/2} \times 3^2 + (27)^{1/3} = 3^x \times 2^y$

$\Rightarrow \qquad 6 \times 9 + 3 = 3^x \times 2^y$

$\Rightarrow \qquad 6 \times 3 = 3^x \times 2^y$

$\Rightarrow \qquad 2 \times 3 \times 3 = 3^x \times 2^y$

$\Rightarrow \qquad 3^2 \times 2^1 = 3^x \times 2^y$

$\Rightarrow \quad x = 2, y = 1$ [by comparing]

10. $10^m \times 10^n \times 10^p = 10^6$

$\Rightarrow \qquad m + n + p = 6$

$\therefore \qquad \dfrac{m + n + p}{3} = \dfrac{6}{3} = 2$

$\therefore$ Average value = 2

11. $(6^{30} + 6^{-30})(6^{30} - 6^{-30})$

$$= (6^{30})^2 - (6^{-30})^2$$

$$[\because (a+b)(a-b) = a^2 - b^2]$$

$$= 6^{60} - 6^{-60} = 3^A \cdot 8^B - 3^{-A} \cdot 8^{-B}$$

$\Rightarrow \qquad (3 \cdot 2)^{60} - (3 \cdot 2)^{-60}$

$$= 3^A \cdot 8^B - 3^{-A} \cdot 8^{-B}$$

$\Rightarrow \quad 3^{60} \cdot (8)^{20} - (3^{-60}) \cdot (8)^{-20}$

$$[\because 2^3 = 8]$$

$$= 3^A \cdot 8^B - 3^{-A} \cdot 8^{-B}$$

On comparing, $A = 60, B = 20$

$\therefore \qquad A + B = 80$

12. $\dfrac{2^{2004} - 2^{2003}}{2^{2004} + 2^{2003}} = \dfrac{2^{2003}(2-1)}{2^{2003}(2+1)} = \dfrac{1}{3}$

13. A. $\left(\dfrac{-3}{2}\right)^3 \times x = \left(\dfrac{4}{27}\right)^{-2}$

$\Rightarrow x = \left(\dfrac{4}{27}\right)^{-2} \times \left(\dfrac{-2}{3}\right)^3$

$= \left(\dfrac{27}{4}\right)^2 \times \left(\dfrac{-2}{3}\right)^3$

$= \dfrac{27 \times 27}{4 \times 4} \times \dfrac{-2 \times -2 \times -2}{3 \times 3 \times 3}$

$= \dfrac{-27}{2} = \dfrac{(-3)^3}{2}$

B. $\dfrac{6^n}{6^{-2}} = 6^3$

$\Rightarrow \quad 6^{n+2} = 6^3$

$\Rightarrow \quad n = 1$

C. $4^{n-1} = \dfrac{1}{4} \cdot 4^y$

$\Rightarrow \quad 4^{n-1} = 4^{y-1}$

$\Rightarrow \quad n - 1 = y - 1$

$\Rightarrow \quad y = n$

D. $-(3)^3 - (-3)^2 + (-2)^2$

$= -27 - 9 + 4$

$= -32$

15. $\left(\dfrac{81}{16}\right)^{-3/4} \times \left[\left(\dfrac{25}{9}\right)^{-3/2} \div \left(\dfrac{5}{2}\right)^{-3}\right]$

$= \left\{\left(\dfrac{3}{2}\right)\right\}^{4 \times \left(-\frac{3}{4}\right)} \times \left[\left(\dfrac{5}{3}\right)^{2 \times \left(-\frac{3}{2}\right)} \div \left(\dfrac{5}{2}\right)^{-3}\right]$

$= \left(\dfrac{3}{2}\right)^{-3} \times \left(\dfrac{5}{3}\right)^{-3} \times \left(\dfrac{5}{2}\right)^3$

$= \left(\dfrac{5}{2}\right)^3 \times \left(\dfrac{2}{3}\right)^3 \times \left(\dfrac{3}{5}\right)^3$

$= \left(\dfrac{5}{2} \times \dfrac{2}{3} \times \dfrac{3}{5}\right)^3$

$= (1)^3 = 1$

16. $\dfrac{9^n \times 3^2 \times (3^{-n/2})^{-2} - (27)^n}{3^{3m} \times 2^3} = \dfrac{1}{27}$

$\Rightarrow \dfrac{3^{2n+2} \times 3^n - 3^{3n}}{3^{3m} \times 2^3} = \left(\dfrac{1}{3}\right)^3$

$\Rightarrow \dfrac{3^{3n+2} - 3^{3n}}{3^{3m}} = \left(\dfrac{2}{3}\right)^3$

$\Rightarrow \dfrac{3^{3n}(9-1)}{3^{3m}} = \left(\dfrac{2}{3}\right)^3$

$\Rightarrow \dfrac{3^{3n}(8)}{3^{3m}} = \dfrac{(2)^3}{(3)^3}$

$\Rightarrow \quad 3^{3n-3m} = 3^{-3}$

$\Rightarrow \quad 3n - 3m = -3$

[by comparing]

$\Rightarrow \quad 3m - 3n = 3$

$\therefore \quad m - n = 1$

17. $\dfrac{8^{x+1}}{2^{x-x}} = 64$

$\Rightarrow \quad \dfrac{8^{x+1}}{2^0} = 64$

$\Rightarrow \quad 8^{x+1} = 8^2 \quad [\because 2^0 = 1]$

On comparing both sides,

$x + 1 = 2$

$\Rightarrow \quad x = 1$

$\therefore \quad 3^{2x+1} = 3^3 = 27$

18. $\sqrt{2\dfrac{1}{4}} \times \left(1\dfrac{1}{3}\right)^2 + 1 \div \sqrt[3]{3\dfrac{3}{8}}$

$= \sqrt{\dfrac{9}{4}} \times \left(\dfrac{4}{3}\right)^2 + 1 \div \left(\dfrac{27}{8}\right)^{1/3}$

$= \left\{\left(\dfrac{3}{2}\right)^2\right\}^{1/2} \times \left(\dfrac{4}{3}\right)^2 + 1 \div \left(\dfrac{3}{2}\right)^{3 \times \frac{1}{3}}$

$= \dfrac{3}{2} \times \dfrac{16}{9} + 1 \div \dfrac{3}{2}$

$= \dfrac{3}{2} \times \dfrac{16}{9} + \dfrac{2}{3}$

$= \dfrac{8}{3} + \dfrac{2}{3} = \dfrac{10}{3} = 3\dfrac{1}{3}$

19. Given, $\dfrac{2 \cdot 3^{n+1} + 7 \cdot 3^{n-1}}{3^{n+2} - 2\left(\dfrac{1}{3}\right)^{1-n}}$

$= \dfrac{2 \cdot 3^{n+1} + 7 \cdot 3^{n-1}}{3^{n+2} - 2(3)^{n-1}}$

$= \dfrac{3^{n-1}(2 \times 3^2 + 7)}{3^{n-1}(3^3 - 2)}$

$= \left(\dfrac{25}{25}\right) = 1$

20. $4^x + 4^x + 4^x + 4^x + 4^x + 4^x + 4^x$

$\qquad\qquad + 4^x = \dfrac{1}{512}$

$\Rightarrow \quad 8 \cdot 4^x = \dfrac{1}{512}$

$\Rightarrow \quad 4^x = \dfrac{1}{512 \times 8}$

$\Rightarrow \quad 2^{2x} = 2^{-12}$

$\Rightarrow \quad 2x = -12 \quad$ [by comparing]

$\Rightarrow \quad x = -6$

$\therefore \quad -\dfrac{3}{x} = \dfrac{-3}{-6} = \dfrac{1}{2} = 0.5$

21. $3^x \times \dfrac{10}{3} - 3^{x-1} = 81$

$\Rightarrow \quad 10 \times 3^{x-1} - 3^{x-1} = 81$

$\Rightarrow \quad 3^{x-1}(10 - 1) = 81$

$\Rightarrow \quad 9 \times 3^{x-1} = 81$

$\Rightarrow \quad 3^{x-1} = 9$

$\Rightarrow \quad 3^{x-1} = 3^2$

$\Rightarrow \quad x - 1 = 2$

[by comparing]

$\therefore \quad x = 3$

22. Let initial number of cells be 1.

After an hour $= 2 \times 1 = 2^1$

After 2 h $= 4 \times 1 = 2^2$

After 10 h $= 2^{10}$

$\therefore$ Number of cells $= 2^{10}$

$\qquad\qquad = 1024$

23.

$\text{I} \xrightarrow{\times 2^{-3}} \text{II} \xrightarrow{\times 12^{-1}} \text{III} \xrightarrow{\times 3^{-2}} 1/6$

Going from right hand side,

$\dfrac{1}{6} \times 3^2 \times 12 \times 2^3$

$= \dfrac{1}{6} \times 9 \times 12 \times 8$

$= 144$

$\therefore$ In IInd circle $= 144 \times 2^{-3}$

$\qquad\qquad = 144 \times \dfrac{1}{8} = 18$

24. Let the input be x.

According to the question,

$x \times 2^2 \times 3^2 \times 6^{-2} \times \left(\dfrac{2}{3}\right)^{-1} + \left(\dfrac{4}{3}\right)^{-1} = 16$

$\Rightarrow \quad \dfrac{x \times 2^2 \times 3^2}{6^2} \times \dfrac{3}{2} \times \dfrac{4}{3} = 16$

$\therefore \quad x = \dfrac{16 \times 6 \times 6 \times 2 \times 3}{2^2 \times 3^2 \times 3 \times 4} = 8$

25. I. True $\qquad\qquad$ II. False

III. True $\qquad\qquad$ IV. False

V. True

26. I. $-\left(\dfrac{1}{2}\right)^5$

II. different

III. $\left(\dfrac{5}{8}\right)$

IV. 3

V. $\dfrac{1}{81}$

Mathematics OLYMPIAD Class VIII

3 Square and Square Root

1. Here, $\sqrt{36} = 6$
$\sqrt{196} = 14$
$\sqrt{169} = 13$
$\sqrt{181} = 13.45$
Hence, 181 is not a perfect square.

2. 7 cannot be the last digit (unit's place) for perfect number.

3. $\because \quad x = \sqrt{169} = 13$
and $\quad y = \sqrt{64} = 8$
$\therefore \quad x - y = 13 - 8 = 5 = E$

4. Number of odd numbers from 1 to 20
$= 1, 3, 5, 7, 9, 11, 13, 15, 17, 19 = 10$
$\therefore \quad$ Sum $= (10)^2 = 100$

5. $\because \quad m = n^2$
$\therefore \quad n = \sqrt{m}$

6. $\sqrt{248 + \sqrt{52 + \sqrt{144}}}$
$= \sqrt{248 + \sqrt{52 + 12}}$
$= \sqrt{248 + \sqrt{64}}$
$= \sqrt{248 + 8}$
$= \sqrt{256} = 16$

7. Here, $\sqrt{4761} = 69$
$\sqrt{47.61} = \sqrt{\dfrac{4761}{100}} = \dfrac{69}{10} = 6.9$
$\sqrt{0.4761} = \sqrt{\dfrac{4761}{10000}} = \dfrac{69}{100} = 0.69$
$\therefore \quad \sqrt{4761} + \sqrt{47.61} + \sqrt{0.4761}$
$= 69 + 6.9 + 0.69$
$= 76.59$

8. In general, Pythagorean triplet is
$(2n, n^2 - 1, n^2 + 1)$.
$\therefore \quad 5 = n^2 + 1$
$\Rightarrow \quad n = 2$
$\therefore \quad 2n = 4$
$\Rightarrow \quad n^2 - 1 = 4 - 1 = 3$
So, the other numbers are 3 and 4.

9. $\because \sqrt{2 + \sqrt{x}} = 3$
Squaring on both sides,
$2 + \sqrt{x} = 9$
$\Rightarrow \quad \sqrt{x} = 7$
$\therefore \quad x = (7)^2 = 49$

10. LCM of $6, 9, 15 = 3 \times 2 \times 3 \times 5$
$= 90$
But we see that, 90 is not a perfect square.
$\sqrt{90} = 3\sqrt{10}$
For a perfect square,
$3\sqrt{10} \times \sqrt{10} = 30$

$\therefore \quad$ Square of $30 = 900$
So, smallest number which is a perfect square, is 900.

11. $\because \sqrt{1 + \dfrac{27}{169}} = \left(1 + \dfrac{x}{13}\right)$
$\Rightarrow \quad \sqrt{\dfrac{169 + 27}{169}} = 1 + \dfrac{x}{13}$
$\Rightarrow \quad \dfrac{14}{13} = 1 + \dfrac{x}{13}$
$\Rightarrow \quad 1 + \dfrac{1}{13} = 1 + \dfrac{x}{13}$
$\therefore \quad x = 1$

12. $\because \quad 80^2 = 6400$
and $\quad 85^2 = 7225$
So, 6800 lies between 80 and 85.
Also, $\quad 81^2 = 6561$
$82^2 = 6724$
$83^2 = 6889 \ldots$ near to 6800.
Hence, 89 must be added.

13. We know that,
Greatest five-digit number $= 99999$
where, $\sqrt{99999} = 316.2261$
But we have to find perfect square, so
$316 \times 316 = 99856$

14. We have, $\sqrt{\dfrac{1.69}{0.0036} \times \dfrac{1.44}{6.76} \times \dfrac{0.25}{1.21}}$
$= \sqrt{\dfrac{1.3 \times 1.3}{0.06 \times 0.06} \times \dfrac{1.2 \times 1.2}{2.6 \times 2.6} \times \dfrac{0.5 \times 0.5}{1.1 \times 1.1}}$
$= \dfrac{1.3}{0.06} \times \dfrac{1.2}{2.6} \times \dfrac{0.5}{1.1} = \dfrac{5}{1.1} = 4.54$

17. $\sqrt{188 + \sqrt{53 + \sqrt{y}}} = 14$
On squaring both sides,
$188 + \sqrt{53 + \sqrt{y}} = 196$
$\Rightarrow \quad \sqrt{53 + \sqrt{y}} = 196 - 188$
$\Rightarrow \quad \sqrt{53 + \sqrt{y}} = 8$
Again, squaring on both sides,
$53 + \sqrt{y} = 64$
$\Rightarrow \quad \sqrt{y} = 64 - 53 = 11$
Again, squaring on both sides,
$y = 121$

18. Consider, $\sqrt{6\sqrt{6\sqrt{6\sqrt{6}}}}$
$= \sqrt{6\sqrt{6\sqrt{6 \times 6^{1/2}}}} = \sqrt{6\sqrt{6\sqrt{6^{3/2}}}}$
$= \sqrt{6\sqrt{6 \times 6^{3/4}}} = \sqrt{6\sqrt{6^{7/4}}}$
$= \sqrt{6 \times 6^{7/8}} = 6^{15/16}$

19. Total amount collected $= ₹ 9216$
Let the number of students be x.
Then, amount contributed by each student $= ₹ x$
According to the question,
$\Rightarrow \quad x \times x = 9216$
$\Rightarrow \quad x^2 = 9216$
$\Rightarrow \quad x = \sqrt{9216}$
$= 96$
$\therefore \quad$ Total number of students $= 96$

20. Given, $\quad a = \sqrt{2} + 1$
and $\quad b = \sqrt{2} - 1$
$\therefore \quad a + b = 2\sqrt{2}$
and $\quad a - b = 2$
Now, $\quad ab = 2 - 1 = 1$
$[\because (a + b)(a - b) = a^2 - b^2]$
$\therefore \quad \dfrac{a^2 - ab + b^2}{a^2 + ab + b^2} = \dfrac{(a - b)^2 + ab}{(a + b)^2 - ab}$
$= \dfrac{(2)^2 + 1}{(2\sqrt{2})^2 - 1}$
$= \dfrac{4 + 1}{8 - 1} = \dfrac{5}{7}$

21. Since, numbers are in the ratio $1 : 2 : 3$.
Let the numbers be $x, 2x$ and $3x$.
According to the question,
$x^2 + (2x)^2 + (3x)^2 = 224$
$\Rightarrow \quad x^2 + 4x^2 + 9x^2 = 224$
$\Rightarrow \quad 14x^2 = 224$
$\Rightarrow \quad x^2 = 16$
$\Rightarrow \quad x = 4$
$\therefore \quad$ Difference between squares of greatest and smallest numbers
$= (3x)^2 - (x)^2$
$= 8x^2 = 8 \times 16 = 128$

22. Total money paid
$= 1 + 3 + 5 + 7 + 9 + \ldots + 30 \text{ terms}$
$= 30^2 = 900$
[since, sum of n consecutive numbers is n^2]
Interest paid $= ₹ 150$
$\therefore \quad$ Amount borrowed $= ₹ (900 - 150)$
$= ₹ 750$

23. I. False   II. False   III. False
IV. False   IV. False

24. I. 144   II. 400   III. $2n + 1$
IV. 8, 15

Cube and Cube Root

1. $1331 = 11 \times 11 \times 11$

$\Rightarrow \quad \sqrt[3]{1331} = 11$

Hence, 1331 is a perfect cube.

2. $\sqrt[3]{(-125) \times (-3375)} = (-5) \times (-15)$
$$= 75$$

3. $1729 = 1728 + 1 = 12^3 + 1^3$

4. $(-9)^3 = -729 \qquad [\because \sqrt[3]{(-\text{ve})} = -\text{ve}]$

5. $\sqrt[3]{27} + \sqrt[3]{0.008} + \sqrt[3]{0.064}$
$$= 3 + 0.2 + 0.4 = 3.6$$

6. $\dfrac{14^3}{15^3} = \dfrac{2744}{3375}$

7. $32 = 2 \times 2 \times 2 \times 2 \times 2$

For making the perfect cube,

we multiply 32 by 2.

So, $K = 2$, i.e. $32 \times 2 = 64 = 4^3$

8. $\sqrt[3]{288} \times \sqrt[3]{432} \times \sqrt[3]{648}$
$$= \sqrt[3]{\frac{(2 \times 3 \times 4 \times 3 \times 4)(2 \times 6 \times 6}{\times 6)(3 \times 6 \times 6 \times 6)}}$$
$$= 6 \times 6 \times 3 \times 4 = 432$$

9. $\because x^2 > y^2$

$\Rightarrow \qquad x > y \, \alpha - x > -y$

$\Rightarrow \qquad x \times x^2 > y \times y^2$

$\Rightarrow \qquad x^3 > y^3$

10. We have, $243 = 3 \times 3 \times 3 \times 3 \times 3$

So, to have a perfect cube root

243 should be divided by 9.

11. LCM of 4, 9 and $12 = 36$

Perfect cube greater than 36 is 64.

$\therefore$ Required number $= 64 - 36 = 28$

13. $\sqrt[3]{3\left(\sqrt[3]{x} - \dfrac{1}{\sqrt[3]{x}}\right)} = 2$

Cubing on both sides,

$$3\left(\sqrt[3]{x} - \frac{1}{\sqrt[3]{x}}\right) = 8$$

$\Rightarrow \qquad \sqrt[3]{x} - \dfrac{1}{\sqrt[3]{x}} = \dfrac{8}{3} \qquad \ldots \text{(i)}$

Cubing both sides, we get

$$x - \frac{1}{x} - 3\left(\sqrt[3]{x} - \frac{1}{\sqrt[3]{x}}\right) = \frac{512}{27}$$

$\Rightarrow x - \dfrac{1}{x} - 3 \times \dfrac{8}{3} = \dfrac{512}{27}$ [from Eq. (i)]

$\Rightarrow x - \dfrac{1}{x} = \dfrac{512}{27} + 8 = \dfrac{728}{27}$

14. Given, numbers are in the ratio $2 : 3 : 4$.

Let the numbers be $2x$, $3x$ and $4x$.

Then, $(2x)^3 + (3x)^3 + (4x)^3 = 33957$

$\Rightarrow \quad 8x^3 + 27x^3 + 64x^3 = 33957$

$\Rightarrow \qquad x^3 = \dfrac{33957}{99} \Rightarrow x^3 = 343$

$\Rightarrow \qquad x = \sqrt[3]{343} = 7$

$\therefore$ Difference in cubes of greatest and

smallest numbers $= (4x)^3 - (2x)^3$
$$= (64 - 8)x^3 = 56x^3$$
$$= 56 \times 7 \times 7 \times 7$$
$$= 343 \times 56 = 19208$$

16. $\because \qquad\qquad x^3 = 4x$

$\Rightarrow \qquad\qquad x^3 - 4x = 0$

$\Rightarrow \qquad\qquad x\,(x^2 - 4) = 0$

Either $x = 0$ or $x^2 - 4 = 0$

$\Rightarrow \qquad\qquad x^2 = 4$

$\Rightarrow \qquad\qquad x = \pm\, 2$

$\because \qquad\qquad x \neq 0,\, x \neq -2$

$\therefore \qquad\qquad x = 2$

17. Surface area of cube $= 6\,l^2$

$\qquad\qquad$ [where, l is a side]

$\Rightarrow \qquad 6\,l^2 = 150$

$\Rightarrow \qquad l^2 = 25 \Rightarrow l = 5$

$\therefore$ Volume $= l^3 = (5)^3 = 125 \text{ cm}^3$

18. In the given figure, except option (d) the
rule followed is

(a) $\{2 \times 3 + 1^3\}^3 = (6 + 1)^3$
$$= 7^3 = 343$$

(b) $\{7 \times 2 + 2^3\}^3 = (14 + 8)^3$
$$= (22)^3 = 10648$$

(c) $\{5 \times 3 + 2^3\}^3 = (15 + 8)^3$
$$= (23)^3 = 12167$$

(d) $\{3 \times 2 + 2^3\}^3 = (6 + 8)^3$
$$= \{14\}^3 \neq 3375$$

19. $1A6B3$

$B = $ Greatest single digit perfect cube $= 8$

$\qquad\qquad A = 2 \times 8 - 7 = 9$

$\therefore \qquad\qquad$ Number $= 19683$

Now, $\quad \sqrt[3]{19683} = 27$

$\therefore$ Sum $= 19683 + 27 = 19710$

21. I. True $\qquad$ II. False $\qquad$ III. False

IV. False $\qquad$ V. True

22. I. $27 \text{ cm}^3 \qquad$ II. 8 $\qquad$ III. 9

IV. 3 $\qquad\qquad$ V. 7, 3

5

Algebraic Expressions

1. Degree of constant polynomial $= 0$

e.g. 2, 7, ... etc, are called constant
polynomials.

3. Degree of $5x^3 y^2 + 6xy^7 - x^6 = 7 + 1$
$$= 8$$

Degree of $4x^5 - 4x^3 + 2 = 5$

$\therefore \qquad$ Difference $= 8 - 5 = 3$

7. $a - b + ab + b + c - bc - a - ac + c$
$$= 2c + ab - bc - ac$$

8. $x^4 + 2x^2 - 3x + 7 - (x^3 + x^2 + x - 1)$
$$= x^4 + 2x^2 - 3x + 7 - x^3 - x^2 - x + 1$$
$$= x^4 - x^3 + x^2 - 4x + 8$$

9. $(x^2 + 3x + 5) \times (x^2 - 1)$
$$= x^2\,(x^2 + 3x + 5) - 1\,(x^2 + 3x + 5)$$
$$= x^4 + 3x^3 + 5x^2 - x^2 - 3x - 5$$
$$= x^4 + 3x^3 + 4x^2 - 3x - 5$$

10. Let length of a rectangle, $l = x$ m

Then, breadth of rectangle,
$$b = (2x - 5) \text{ m}$$

$\therefore$ Perimeter $= 2(l + b) = 2(x + 2x - 5)$
$$= 2(3x - 5) = 6x - 10$$

11. Given, perimeter of a triangle is 20 m and
sides are in the ratio $2 : 3 : 5$.

$\therefore \quad 2x + 3x + 5x = 20 \Rightarrow x = 2$ m

$\therefore$ Difference between longest and
smallest sides $= (5 - 2)x = 3 \times 2 = 6$ m

12.
$$y - 2 \overline{)\,y^3 - 6y^2 + 9y - 2\,}\,(y^2 - 4y + 1$$
$$\underline{y^3 - 2y^2}$$
$$-\quad +$$
$$-4y^2 + 9y - 2$$
$$\underline{-4y^2 + 8y}$$
$$+\quad -$$
$$y - 2$$
$$\underline{y - 2}$$
$$0$$

$\therefore \qquad$ Quotient $= y^2 - 4y + 1$

13.
$$m^2 - 3m + 4 \overline{)\,5m^3 - 13m^2 + 15m + 7\,}\,(5m + 2$$
$$5m^3 - 15m^2 + 20m$$
$$\underline{-\quad + \quad -}$$
$$2m^2 - 5m + 7$$
$$2m^2 - 6m + 8$$
$$\underline{-\quad + \quad -}$$
$$m - 1$$

$\therefore$ Remainder $= m - 1$

14. A. $4x^2 - 20xy + 25y^2$
$$= (2x)^2 - 2 \cdot 2x \cdot 5y + (5y)^2$$
$$[\because a^2 - 2ab + b^2 = (a - b)^2$$
$$= (a - b)\,(a - b)]$$
$$= (2x - 5y)\,(2x - 5y)$$

B. $(x + a)\,(x + b) = x^2 + (a + b)x + ab$

$\because \quad a = 2, b = 3 \qquad\qquad$ [given]
$$= x^2 + (2 + 3)x + 2 \times 3$$
$$= x^2 + 5x + 6$$

C. $34 \times 26 = (30 + 4)\,(30 - 4)$
$$\Rightarrow (a + b)\,(a - b) \text{ or } (x + b)\,(x - b)$$

D. $(21x - 13y)(21x - 13y)$
$$= (21x)^2 - 2 \cdot 21x \cdot 13y + (13y)^2$$
$$= 441x^2 - 546xy + 169y^2$$

15. Area of square $= 625\,m^2$ [given]
$$\therefore \qquad (4x + 5)(4x + 5) = 625$$
$$\Rightarrow \qquad (4x + 5)^2 = 625$$
$$\Rightarrow \qquad (4x + 5)^2 = (25)^2$$
$$[\because \sqrt{625} \neq -25]$$
$$\Rightarrow \quad 4x + 5 = 25 \Rightarrow x = 5$$
$$\therefore \quad \text{Perimeter} = 4(4x + 5) = 4 \times 25$$
$$= 100\,m$$

16. Area of rectangle $= x^2 + 7x + 12$
Breadth $= ?$
Length $= (x + 3)$
We know that,
Area of rectangle
$$= \text{Length} \times \text{Breadth}$$
$$(x^2 + 7x + 12) = (x + 3) \times \text{Breadth}$$
$$\Rightarrow (x^2 + 7x + 12) \div (x + 3) = \text{Breadth}$$
$$\Rightarrow (x + 4)(x + 3) \div (x + 3) = \text{Breadth}$$
$$\Rightarrow x + 4 = \text{Breadth}$$
$$\therefore \text{Breadth} = 2 + 4 = 6 \quad [\because x = 2, \text{given}]$$

17. $p^2 + q^2 = ?$
$$\because \quad p + q = 12, p \cdot q = 22 \quad [\text{given}]$$
Consider $\quad p + q = 12$
On squaring both sides, we get
$$p^2 + q^2 + 2pq = 144$$
$$\Rightarrow \quad p^2 + q^2 + 2 \times 22 = 144$$
$$\Rightarrow \qquad p^2 + q^2 = 100$$

18. Given,
$$m - n = 16, m^2 + n^2 = 400$$
Consider $m - n = 16$
On squaring both sides, we get
$$(m - n)^2 = (16)^2$$
$$\Rightarrow \quad m^2 + n^2 - 2mn = 256$$
$$\Rightarrow \qquad 400 - 2mn = 256$$
$$\Rightarrow \qquad 2mn = 400 - 256$$
$$\therefore \qquad mn = \frac{144}{2} = 72$$

19. $x - \dfrac{1}{x} = 7 \Rightarrow \left(x - \dfrac{1}{x}\right)^2 = (7)^2$
$$[\text{squaring both sides}]$$
$$\Rightarrow \quad x^2 + \frac{1}{x^2} - 2 \cdot x \cdot \frac{1}{x} = 49$$
$$\Rightarrow \quad x^2 + \frac{1}{x^2} = 49 + 2$$
$$\Rightarrow \quad x^2 + \frac{1}{x^2} = 51$$

20. $\dfrac{6.25 \times 6.25 - 1.75 \times 1.75}{4.5}$
$$= \frac{(6.25)^2 - (1.75)^2}{(6.25 - 1.75)}$$
$$= \frac{(6.25 + 1.75)(6.25 - 1.75)}{(6.25 - 1.75)}$$
$$[\because a^2 - b^2 = (a + b)(a - b)]$$
$$= 6.25 + 1.75 = 8$$

21. Let number be y.
According to the question,
$$y + \frac{1}{y} = 14, y^3 + \frac{1}{y^3} = ?$$
$$\left(y + \frac{1}{y}\right)^3 = (14)^3 \quad [\text{cubic both sides}]$$
$$\Rightarrow y^3 + \frac{1}{y^3} = \left(y + \frac{1}{y}\right)^3 - 3 \cdot y \cdot \frac{1}{y}$$
$$\left(y + \frac{1}{y}\right)$$
$$[\because a^3 + b^3 = (a + b)^3 - 3ab(a + b)]$$
$$= (14)^3 - 3(14)$$
$$= 2744 - 42 = 2702$$

22. $\dfrac{2x^3 - 12x^2 + 16x}{(x - 2)(x - 4)}$
$$= \frac{2x(x^2 - 6x + 8)}{x^2 - 6x + 8} = 2x$$

23. $\because 6^2 + 8^2 = 36 + 64 = 100 = 10^2$
and $a^2 + b^2 = (a + b)^2 - 2ab$
$$\neq (a + b)^2$$

24. Consider $\left(2 + \dfrac{4}{x}\right)\left(10 - \dfrac{15}{x} + \dfrac{25}{x^2}\right)$
$$= (2 + 4)(10 - 15 + 25) \qquad [\because x = 1]$$
$$= (6)(20) = 120$$

25. Consider $(x + 2)^3 - (x - 2)^3$
$$= x^3 + 2^3 + 6x(x + 2) - x^3 + 2^3$$
$$\qquad\qquad\qquad\qquad + 6x(x - 2)$$
$$= 2^3 + 6x^2 + 2^3 + 6x^2 - 12x + 12x$$
$$= 8 + 12x^2 + 8 = 12x^2 + 16$$

26. I. Given, $x^2 + y^2 = 40, xy = 2$
$$\therefore (x - y)^2 = x^2 + y^2 - 2xy$$
$$\Rightarrow (x - y)^2 = 40 - 2 \times 2 = 36$$
$$\therefore \quad x - y = \sqrt{36} = 6$$
II. $(x + a)(x + b) = x^2 + (a + b)x + ab$
III. 0
IV. $x + \dfrac{1}{x} = 9$
On squaring both sides, we get
$$\left(x + \frac{1}{x}\right)^2 = (9)^2$$
$$\Rightarrow \quad x^2 + \frac{1}{x^2} + 2 \times x \times \frac{1}{x} = 81$$
$$\Rightarrow \quad x^2 + \frac{1}{x^2} = 81 - 2 = 79$$
$$\Rightarrow \quad \left(x^2 + \frac{1}{x^2}\right) = 79$$
V. 4

27. I. False   II. True   III. False
IV. False   V. True

28. Perimeter of the triangle $= 8p^2 - 9p + 9$
$\therefore$ Perimeter of a triangle $=$ Sum of the
length of all three sides
i.e. length of first side + length of second
side + length of third side
So, $8p^2 - 9p + 9 = 2p^2 - 3p + 1 + 5p^2$
$$-p + 4 + \text{Length of third side}$$
Length of third side $= 8p^2 - 9p + 9$
$$- (7p^2 - 4p + 5)$$
$$= 8p^2 - 9p + 9 - 7p^2 + 4p - 5$$
$$= p^2 - 5p + 4$$

⑥ *Factorisation of Algebraic Expressions*

1. $6 - y - 2y^2 = -(2y^2 + y - 6)$
$$= -(2y^2 + 4y - 3y - 6)$$
$$= -\{2y(y + 2) - 3(y + 2)\}$$
$$= -\{(2y - 3)(y + 2)\}$$
$$= (y + 2)(-2y + 3)$$
or $(2y - 3)(-y - 2)$

2. $x^3 - 27 = (x)^3 - (3)^3$
$$= (x - 3)(x^2 + 3x + 9)$$
$$[\because a^3 - b^3 = (a - b)(a^2 + ab + b^2)]$$

3. $10x^2 + 21x + 9 = (2x + 3)(5x + 3)$
Put $x = 10$ in both sides, we get
$$10 \cdot (10)^2 + 21 \cdot (10) + 9$$
$$= (2 \times 10 + 3)(5 \times 10 + 3)$$
$$\Rightarrow 1000 + 210 + 9 = 23 \times 53$$
$$\Rightarrow 1219 = 23 \times 53$$

4. $4x^2 - 12xy + 9y^2 = 0$
$$\Rightarrow (2x)^2 + (3y)^2 - 2 \cdot 2x \cdot 3y = 0$$
$$\Rightarrow \qquad (2x - 3y)^2 = 0$$
$$[\because a^2 + b^2 - 2ab = (a - b)(a - b)]$$
$$\Rightarrow \qquad 2x - 3y = 0$$
$$\Rightarrow \qquad 2x = 3y$$
$$\Rightarrow \qquad \frac{2x}{3y} = 1$$

5. $xy - pq + qy - px$
$$= xy - px - pq + qy$$
$$= x(y - p) + q(-p + y)$$
$$= x(y - p) + q(y - p)$$
$$= (x + q)(y - p)$$

6. $x^4 - (x - z)^4$
$$= \{x^2\}^2 - \{(x - z)^2\}^2$$
$$= \{x^2 - (x - z)^2\}\{(x^2 + (x - z)^2\}$$
$$[\because a^2 - b^2 = (a - b)(a + b)]$$
$$= \{(x - x + z)(x + x - z)\}$$
$$\qquad\qquad\qquad \{x^2 + (x - z)^2\}$$
$$= z(2x - z)\{x^2 + (x - z)^2\}$$

7. $\dfrac{58^2 - 42^2}{16} = \dfrac{58^2 - 42^2}{58 - 42}$
$$= \frac{(58 + 42)(58 - 42)}{(58 - 42)} = 100$$

8. $y^2 + 18y + 65 = ay^2 + 2by + 65$
On comparing, we get
$$a = 1, 2b = 18 \Rightarrow b = 9$$
$$\therefore \quad \frac{a + b}{a - b} = \frac{1 + 9}{1 - 9} = -\frac{10}{8} = -\frac{5}{4}$$

ANSWERS AND EXPLANATIONS   **53**

9. $(x^3y^3 + x^2y^3 - xy^4 + xy) \div xy$
$= (x^2y^2 + xy^2 - y^3 + 1)\, xy \div xy$
$= x^2y^2 + xy^2 - y^3 + 1$
$= xy^2 (x + 1) - (y^3 - 1)$
$= xy^2 (x + 1) - (y - 1)(y^2 + y + 1)$
So, we can't factorise.

11. $x^2 + \dfrac{1}{x^2} + 2 - 2x - \dfrac{2}{x}$
$= (x)^2 + \left(\dfrac{1}{x}\right)^2 + 2 \cdot x \cdot \dfrac{1}{x} - 2\left(x + \dfrac{1}{x}\right)$
$= \left(x + \dfrac{1}{x}\right)\left(x + \dfrac{1}{x}\right) - 2\left(x + \dfrac{1}{x}\right)$
$= \left(x + \dfrac{1}{x}\right)\left(x + \dfrac{1}{x} - 2\right)$

12. I. $x^2 - 13x + 42$
II. $x^2 - 7x - 6x + 42$
III. $x(x - 7) - 6(x - 7)$
IV. $(x - 7)(x - 6)$
$\therefore$ Step III is incorrect.

13. The given factorisation shows that the method of algebraic identity is being used.
i.e. $a^2 + 2ab + b^2 = (a + b)^2$
$= (a + b)(a + b)$

14. $6x^2 - 30x + 36$
Student found factors as $(x + 3)(x + 2)$
$= x^2 + 5x + 6$
$= 6x^2 + 30x + 36$ [multiply by 6]
But, we have
$6x^2 - 30x + 36 = 6[x^2 - 5x + 6]$
$= 6[x^2 - 3x - 2x + 6]$
$= 6[(x - 3)(x - 2)]$
$\therefore$ Factors are $(x - 3)(x - 2)$.

15. $(x^2 + 3x + 5)(x^2 - 3x + 5) = m^2 - n^2$
$LHS = (x^2 + 5 + 3x)(x^2 + 5 - 3x)$
$= \{(x^2 + 5) + (3x)\}$
$\qquad \{(x^2 + 5) - (3x)\}$
$RHS = m^2 - n^2 = (m + n)(m - n)$
Here, $m + n = (x^2 + 5) + (3x)$
[by comparing]
$\therefore \qquad m = x^2 + 5$ and $n = 3x$

16. A. $x^2 - 4x + 4$
$= (x)^2 + (2)^2 - 2 \cdot x \cdot 2 = (x - 2)^2$
$[\because (a - b)^2 = a^2 - 2ab + b^2]$
Perfect square
B. $x^2 - 5x + 6 = x^2 - 3x - 2x + 6$
$= (x - 3)(x - 2)$
C. $x^2 - 9x + 18 = x^2 - 6x - 3x + 18$
$= (x - 6)(x - 3)$
D. $3x^2 - 24x + 36$
$= 3\{x^2 - 8x + 12\}$
$= 3\{x^2 - 6x - 2x + 12\}$
$= 3\{(x - 6)(x - 2)\}$
Except (A), all (rest) three are factorised by splitting the middle term. Also, (A) is a complete square.

17. $\dfrac{0.87 \times 0.87 \times 0.87 + 0.13 \times 0.13 \times 0.13}{0.87 + 0.13}$
$= \dfrac{(0.87)^3 + (0.13)^3}{(0.87 + 0.13)}$
$\Rightarrow \dfrac{(0.87 + 0.13)\{(0.87)^2 - (0.87)(0.13) + (0.13)^2\}}{(0.87 + 0.13)}$
$= p\,(0.87)^2 + q(0.87 \times 0.13) + r(0.13)^2$
On comparing both sides, we get
$p = 1, q = -1, r = 1$
$\therefore\ p - q - r = 1 - (-1) - 1$
$= 2 - 1 = 1$

18. Area of rectangular wall
$= 5x \times (5x + 2)$ sq units
$= 25x^2 + 10x$ sq units
Area of door $= 3x \times x = 3x^2$ sq units
Area of window $= 2x \times x$
$= 2x^2$ sq units
$\therefore$ Area to be painted = Total area
$\qquad$ –Area of (door + window)
$= 25x^2 + 10x - 3x^2 - 2x^2$
$= 20x^2 + 10x$ sq units
According to the question,
$5[20x^2 + 10x] = 50$
$\Rightarrow \qquad 2x^2 + x - 1 = 0$

$\Rightarrow \qquad 2x^2 + 2x - x - 1 = 0$
$\Rightarrow \qquad 2x(x + 1) - 1(x + 1) = 0$
$\Rightarrow \qquad (2x - 1)(x + 1) = 0$
Either $x = -1$ or $x = \dfrac{1}{2}$
$\Rightarrow \quad x = \dfrac{1}{2}$ $\qquad$ [neglecting $-ve$]
$\therefore$ Length of wall $= 5 \times \dfrac{1}{2} = \dfrac{5}{2}$
Breadth of wall $= 5 \times \dfrac{1}{2} + 2 = \dfrac{9}{2}$
$\therefore$ Perimeter $= 2\,(5/2 + 9/2)$
$= 14$ units

19. I. $8x^2 - 18x + 9 = (4x - 3) \times (2x - 3)$
II. $8x^2 + 6x$
III. $x + \dfrac{1}{x} = 5$ $\qquad$ [given]
On cubing both sides, we get
$x^3 + \dfrac{1}{x^3} + 3 \cdot x \cdot \dfrac{1}{x}\left(x + \dfrac{1}{x}\right) = 125$
$\Rightarrow \quad x^3 + \dfrac{1}{x^3} = 125 - 3 \times 1 \times 5$
$= 110$
IV. Area of square field
$= 16x^2 + 9y^2 - 24xy$
$= (4x)^2 + (3y)^2 - 2 \cdot 4x \cdot 3y$
$= (4x - 3y)^2$
$\therefore$ Side of field $= \sqrt{(4x - 3y)^2}$
$= 4x - 3y$
$\therefore$ Perimeter $= 4 \times (4x - 3y)$
$= 16x - 12y$
V. $\because m + n = 45$ $\qquad$ ... (i)
and $m^2 - n^2 = 45$ $\qquad$ [given]
$\Rightarrow (m + n)(m - n) = 45$
$\Rightarrow \qquad m - n = \dfrac{45}{45} = 1$ $\qquad$ ... (ii)
From Eqs. (i) and (ii), we get
$m = 23, n = 22$

20. I. True $\qquad$ II. True $\qquad$ III. False
IV. False $\qquad$ V. True

 7 *Linear Equation in One Variable*

1. Let the linear equations in one variable be
$2x = 6, y + 5 = 10, ...$
Here, maximum power of variable must be 1.

2. Given, $\dfrac{x - 2}{x + 3} = \dfrac{3}{8}$
$\Rightarrow \qquad 8x - 16 = 3x + 9 \Rightarrow 5x = 25$
$\therefore \qquad x = 5$

3. Given, $\dfrac{7x + 5}{8x + 6} = \dfrac{2}{3}$
$\therefore \qquad 3(7x + 5) = 2(8x + 6)$

4. (a) $6x - 3 = 3x - 5 \Rightarrow 3x = -2$
$\therefore \qquad x = -\dfrac{2}{3}$

(b) $x - 3 = x + 4$
No solution.
(c) $5x - 3 = 3x - 7$
$\Rightarrow \qquad 2x = -4$
$\therefore \qquad x = -2$
(d) $7x - 6 = 6x - 5 \Rightarrow x = 1$

5. $\because \dfrac{a - 8}{5} = \dfrac{a - 6}{3}$ $\qquad$ [given]
$\Rightarrow \quad 3a - 24 = 5a - 30 \Rightarrow 2a = 6$
$\therefore \qquad a = 3$

7. $(1 + x)$ is a linear expression.

8. $(2x - 2)^2 = 4x^2 + 4x - 4$
$\Rightarrow \quad 4x^2 - 8x + 4 = 4x^2 + 4x - 4$
$\Rightarrow \quad -8x + 4 = 4x - 4$
which is linear equation in one variable.

9. Shyam's age 3 yr hence $= x$ yr
$\therefore$ Shyam's present age $= (x - 3)$ yr
According to the question,
Raju's present age $= 3(x - 3) + 5$
$= (3x - 4)$ yr
Now, $(x - 3) + (3x - 4) = 25$
$\Rightarrow \qquad 4x = 32 \Rightarrow x = 8$
$\therefore$ Raju's present age
$= 3 \times 8 - 4 = 20$ yr

10. Let first (smallest) number be x.
$\therefore \qquad$ Second number $= x + 9$
$\qquad\qquad$ Third number $= x + 18$
$\qquad\qquad$ Fourth number $= x + 27$

MATHEMATICS OLYMPIAD CLASS VIII

According to the question,
$$x + x + 9 + x + 18 + x + 27 = 270$$
$$\Rightarrow \quad 4x + 54 = 270$$
$$\Rightarrow \quad 4x = 216 \Rightarrow x = 54$$
$\therefore$ Average of the numbers
$$= \frac{270}{4} = 67.5$$

11. Let the number be x.
According to the question,
$$\left(\frac{2}{3}\right) x \times \frac{3}{4} = 6$$
$$\Rightarrow \quad \frac{6}{12} x = 6 \Rightarrow x = \frac{6 \times 12}{6}$$
$$\therefore \qquad\qquad x = 12$$

12. Given equation is
$$\frac{x}{3} - \frac{1}{4}\left(x - \frac{1}{2}\right) = \frac{1}{8}(x + 1) + \frac{1}{12}$$
$$\Rightarrow \quad \frac{x}{3} - \frac{x}{4} + \frac{1}{8} = \frac{1}{8}x + \frac{1}{8} + \frac{1}{12}$$
$$\Rightarrow \quad \frac{x}{3} - \frac{x}{4} - \frac{x}{8} = \frac{1}{12}$$
$$\Rightarrow \quad \frac{8x - 6x - 3x}{24} = \frac{1}{12}$$
$$\Rightarrow \quad \frac{-x}{24} = \frac{1}{12}$$
$$\therefore \qquad\qquad x = -2$$

14. According to the question,
$$y = x + 5$$
$$\therefore \qquad 3x + 2y = 75 \qquad \text{[given]}$$
$$\Rightarrow \quad 3x + 2(x + 5) = 75$$
$$\Rightarrow \quad 3x + 2x + 10 = 75$$
$$\Rightarrow \qquad\qquad 5x = 65$$
$$\therefore \qquad\qquad x = 13$$

15. Let man's age be x yr.
Wife's age $= (x - 9)$ yr
Now, according to the question,
$$x + x - 9 = 99$$
$$\Rightarrow \qquad\qquad 2x = 108$$
$$\therefore \qquad\qquad x = 54$$
$$\therefore \qquad \text{Man's age} = 54 \text{ yr}$$
and wife's age $= 45$ yr
[both are numerically same, also same digits are reversed]

16. Let the breadth of rectangle be x m.
$\therefore$ Length of rectangle $= (3x - 6)$ m
Now, perimeter $= 148$ m
The perimeter of new rectangle
$$= 2 \times 148 = 296 \text{ m}$$
$$\therefore \quad 2(x + 3x - 6) = 296$$
$$\Rightarrow \qquad 4x - 6 = 148$$
$$\Rightarrow \qquad\qquad 4x = 154$$
$$\Rightarrow \qquad\qquad x = 38.5 \text{ m}$$
$$\therefore \quad \text{Length} = 3 \times 38.5 - 6$$
$$= 115.5 - 6 = 109.5 \text{ m}$$
and breadth $= x$ m $= 38.5$ m

17. Let the numerator of a rational number be x.
$\therefore$ Denominator of a rational number $= x + 2$
$$\therefore \qquad \text{Number} = \frac{x}{x + 2}$$
According to the question,
$$\frac{x - 2}{x + 2 + 2} = \frac{1}{3}$$
$$\Rightarrow \quad 3x - 6 = x + 4 \Rightarrow 2x = 10$$
$$\therefore \qquad\qquad x = 5$$
$$\therefore \quad \text{Rational number} = \frac{5}{5 + 2} = \frac{5}{7}$$

18. Let two years ago,
Age of son $= x$ yr
$\therefore$ Age of Mohan $= 3x$ yr
After two years, the age of son
$$= x + 2 + 2 = (x + 4) \text{ yr}$$
and age of Mohan $= (3x + 4)$ yr
According to the question,
$$2(3x + 4) = 5(x + 4)$$
$$\Rightarrow \quad 6x + 8 = 5x + 20$$
$$\therefore \qquad\qquad x = 12$$
$\therefore$ Present age of Mohan
$$= 3x + 2 = 38 \text{ yr}$$

19. (a) $\dfrac{3x - 5}{6} = \dfrac{x}{3} \Rightarrow 9x - 15 = 6x$
$$\Rightarrow 3x = 15 \Rightarrow x = 5$$
(b) $\dfrac{z}{3} - \dfrac{1}{3} = \dfrac{4}{3} \Rightarrow \dfrac{z - 1}{3} = \dfrac{4}{3} \Rightarrow z = 5$
(c) $6y + 7 = 3y + 22$
$$\Rightarrow 6y - 3y = 22 - 7 \Rightarrow 3y = 15$$
$$\Rightarrow y = 15$$
(d) $\dfrac{7y - 1}{4} = \dfrac{10}{3} \Rightarrow 21y - 3 = 40$
$$\Rightarrow 21y = 43 \Rightarrow y = \frac{43}{21}$$

20. Let the number be x.
According to the question,
$$x \times \frac{1}{5} + 30 = \frac{x}{4} - 30$$
$$\Rightarrow \qquad \frac{x}{5} + 30 = \frac{x}{4} - 30$$
$$\Rightarrow \qquad \frac{x}{4} - \frac{x}{5} = 60 \Rightarrow \frac{x}{20} = 60$$
$$\therefore \qquad\qquad x = 1200$$

21. Perimeter of rectangle $= 240$ cm [given]
Let length of rectangle be x cm.
$\therefore$ Breadth of rectangle $= (120 - x)$ cm
Since, length is increased by 10%.
$$\therefore \quad \text{New length} = x + x \times \frac{10}{100} = \frac{11x}{10}$$
New breadth
$$= (120 - x) - (120 - x) \times \frac{20}{100}$$
$$= \frac{600 - 5x - 120 + x}{5} = \frac{480 - 4x}{5}$$

Also, the perimeter is same i.e. 240 cm.
$$\therefore \quad \frac{11x}{10} + \frac{480 - 4x}{5} = 120$$
$$\Rightarrow \quad 11x + 960 - 8x = 120 \times 10$$
$$\Rightarrow \qquad 3x = 240 \Rightarrow x = 80$$
$\therefore$ Length of rectangle $= 80$ cm
and breadth of rectangle $= 120 - 80$
$$= 40 \text{ cm}$$

22. (a) $\dfrac{x}{3} - \dfrac{x}{2} = 8 \Rightarrow \dfrac{12}{3} - \dfrac{12}{2} = 8$
$$[\because x = 12, \text{ given}]$$
$$\Rightarrow \qquad 4 - 6 = 8 \Rightarrow -2 \neq 8$$
(b) $\dfrac{x}{3} - \dfrac{x}{4} = 16 \quad \Rightarrow \quad \dfrac{12}{3} - \dfrac{12}{4} = 16$
$$[\because x = 12, \text{ given}]$$
$$\Rightarrow 4 - 3 = 16 \Rightarrow 1 \neq 16$$
(c) $\dfrac{x}{2} + \dfrac{x}{3} - \dfrac{x}{4} = 7$
$$\Rightarrow \qquad \frac{12}{2} + \frac{12}{3} - \frac{12}{4} = 7$$
$$[\because x = 12, \text{ given}]$$
$$\Rightarrow \quad 6 + 4 - 3 = 7 \Rightarrow 7 = 7$$
(d) $\dfrac{2x}{3} = \dfrac{8}{12} - \dfrac{0.25}{3}$
$$\Rightarrow \frac{2 \times 12}{3} = \frac{8}{12} - \frac{0.25}{3}$$
$$[\because x = 12, \text{ given}]$$
$$\Rightarrow \quad 8 = \frac{2}{3} - \frac{0.25}{3} \Rightarrow 8 = \frac{1.75}{3}$$
$$\Rightarrow \qquad 24 \neq 1.75$$

23. I. False   II. False   III. False
IV. False   V. True
$$\frac{x}{2} + \frac{x}{5} + \frac{3x}{10} = \frac{1}{5} + \frac{4}{5}$$
$$\Rightarrow \quad 5x + 2x + 3x = 10 \Rightarrow 10x = 10$$
$$\therefore \qquad\qquad x = 1$$
Hence, $x = 1$ is a solution of given equation.

24. I. highest
II. $p \times 5 - 9 = 11 \Rightarrow 5p = 20 \Rightarrow p = 4$
III. Let number of paneer tikkas be x.
Number of pastries $= x$
$$\therefore \quad x \times 9 + x \times 9 \times \frac{2}{3} = 300$$
$$\Rightarrow \quad 9x + 6x = 300 \Rightarrow 15x = 300$$
$$\Rightarrow \qquad\qquad x = 20$$
$\therefore$ Number of paneer tikkas
$$= \text{Number of pastries} = 20$$
IV. solution
V. $\dfrac{2}{5x} - \dfrac{5}{3x} = \dfrac{1}{15}$ [given]
$$\Rightarrow \qquad \frac{6 - 25}{15x} = \frac{1}{15}$$
$$\Rightarrow \qquad \frac{-19}{15x} = \frac{1}{15}$$
$$\therefore \qquad\qquad x = -19$$

$\textbf{8}$ Profit, Loss and Discount

2. Profit/loss is always calculate on CP.

3. CP = ₹10

Gain per cent = 10%
$$= 10 \times \frac{10}{100} = 1$$

∴ Selling price = 10 + 1 = ₹ 11

4. SP = ₹ 1085

Profit per cent = $8\frac{1}{2}$%

CP = ?

By using the formula,
$$CP = \frac{SP \times 100}{100 + Profit\%}$$

∴ CP = $\dfrac{1085 \times 100}{100 + 8.5}$

$$= \frac{1085 \times 100}{108.5}$$

$$= ₹ 1000$$

5. Use formula for successive discount for x%, y% and z%.

First, $x + y - \dfrac{x \times y}{100} \to r\%$ [say]

Then, r% and z%
$$\left(r + z - \frac{r \times z}{100} \right)\%$$

So, $r\% = 20 + 10 - \dfrac{20 \times 10}{100} = 28\%$

∴ Final discount
$$= 28 + 10 - \frac{28 \times 10}{100} = 38 - 2.8$$
$$= 35.2\%$$

6. CP of 5 oranges = ₹ 6

Profit per cent = 20%

∴ SP of 5 oranges = $6 + 6 \times \dfrac{20}{100}$

$$= 6 + 1.2$$
$$= ₹ 7.2$$

∴ SP of 1 orange = $₹ \dfrac{7.2}{5} = ₹ 1.44$

7. Marked price of an article = ₹ 500

Discount per cent = 5%

∴ SP of article
$$= ₹ \left(500 - 500 \times \frac{5}{100} \right)$$
$$= ₹ 475$$

Profit per cent = 25%

∴ CP of article = $\dfrac{475 \times 100}{100 + 25}$

$$= \frac{475 \times 100}{125} = ₹ 380$$

8. CP of 1 lemon = $\dfrac{48}{12} = ₹ 4$

SP of 1 lemon = $\dfrac{40}{10} = ₹ 4$

∴ CP = SP

i.e. no loss or profit during this transaction.

9. Let marked price of a pen be ₹ 100.

Discount = 20%

∴ SP = $₹ \left(100 - 100 \times \dfrac{20}{100} \right)$

$$= ₹ 80$$

New marked price
$$= 100 + 100 \times \frac{20}{100}$$
$$= ₹120$$

Discount allowed = 20%

∴ New SP = $₹ \left(120 - 120 \times \dfrac{20}{100} \right)$

$$= ₹ 96$$

Now, change in SP = ₹(96 − 80)
$$= ₹16$$

∴ Per cent change in SP = $\dfrac{16}{80} \times 100$
$$= 20\%$$

11. Let cost price of A be ₹ 100.

∴ SP of A = CP of B
$$= ₹100 + \left(₹100 \times \frac{30}{100} \right) = ₹130$$

∴ SP of B = CP of C
$$= ₹130 - \left(₹130 \times \frac{20}{100} \right) = ₹104$$

If C pays ₹ 104, then CP of A is ₹ 100.

∴ C pays ₹ 520, then CP of A
$$= ₹ \frac{100 \times 520}{104} = ₹ 500$$

12. Stores A and B charge for video game = ₹ 750

For store B,

SP of video game = ₹ 600

For store A,

SP of video game
$$= ₹ 750 - \left(₹ 750 \times \frac{25}{100} \right)$$
$$= ₹ 562.5$$

So, store A provides video game at less price.

13. Let CP of radio be ₹ 100.

SP of radio = ₹(100 − 100 × 2.5%)
$$= ₹ 97.5$$

SP, if profit = 7.5%

SP = 100 + 100 × 7.5 %
$$= 100 + 100 \times \frac{7.5}{100}$$
$$= ₹107.5$$

∴ Difference in SP = ₹ 10

When difference is ₹ 10, CP of radio ₹ 100.

When difference is ₹ 100, CP of radio = $₹ \dfrac{100 \times 100}{10} = ₹ 1000$

Profit per cent = 12.5%

∴ SP = $1000 + 1000 \times \dfrac{12.5}{100}$

$$= ₹ 1125$$

14. CP of 20 dozens notebooks
$$= ₹ 48 \times 20 = ₹ 960$$

CP of 8 dozens notebooks
$$= ₹ 48 \times 8 = ₹ 384$$

SP of 8 dozens notebooks
$$= ₹ \left(384 + 384 \times \frac{10}{100} \right)$$
$$= ₹ 422.4$$

CP of 12 dozens notebooks
$$= ₹ 48 \times 12 = ₹ 576$$

SP of 12 dozens notebooks
$$= ₹ \left(576 + 576 \times \frac{20}{100} \right)$$
$$= ₹ 691.2$$

∴ Total SP = ₹ (422.4 + 691.2)
$$= ₹ 1113.6$$

Profit = ₹ (1113.6 − 960) = ₹ 153.6

∴ Profit per cent = $₹ \dfrac{153.6}{960} \times 100$

$$= 16\%$$

15. In option (c) there is loss and in all other cases, there is profit.

16. For A marked an article is ₹ 5000.

Successive discount for A,
$$x + y - \frac{xy}{100} = 20 + 40 - \frac{20 \times 40}{100}$$
$$= 60 - \frac{800}{100} = 52\%$$

∴ Selling price = $5000 - 5000 \times \dfrac{52}{100}$

$$= 5000 - 2600 = ₹2400$$

For B marked an article is ₹ 5000.

Selling price = $5000 - 5000 \times \dfrac{60}{100}$

$$= 5000 - 3000 = ₹2000$$

For C marked an article is ₹ 5000.

Successive discount for C,
$$x + y - \frac{x \times y}{100} = 30 + 30 - \frac{30 \times 30}{100}$$
$$= 60 - \frac{900}{100} = 51\%$$

∴ Selling price = $5000 - 5000 \times \dfrac{51}{100}$

$$= 5000 - 2550$$
$$= ₹2450$$

Thus, maximum selling price is ₹ 2450.

17. I. False II. False

III. True IV. True

V. False

18. I. Sales tax II. 4.5

III. $11\dfrac{1}{9}$% IV. 1000

V. 199.5

⑨ *Simple and Compound Interest*

2. Let the principal be P in case of SI.

$r = r\%, T = 2$ yr, amount $= 2P$

$SI = 2P - P = P$

$\therefore \quad P = \dfrac{P \times r \times 2}{100} \qquad \left[\because SI = \dfrac{PRT}{100}\right]$

$\Rightarrow \quad r = 50\%$

In case of compound interest,

$\qquad r = R\%, t = 2$ yr, $A = 2P$

Using formula, $A = P\left[1 + \dfrac{r}{100}\right]^t$

$\therefore \quad 2P = P\left[1 + \dfrac{R}{100}\right]^2$

$\Rightarrow \quad 2 = \left(1 + \dfrac{R}{100}\right)^2$

$\Rightarrow 1 + \dfrac{R}{100} = \sqrt{2} = 1.41$

$\Rightarrow \quad R = 0.41 \times 100 = 41\%$

i.e. $\quad r > R$

3. Number of times interest changed

$\qquad = 3 \times 4 = 12 \qquad [\because 1 \text{ yr} = 4 \text{ quarters}]$

4. Let sum borrowed be P.

Amount paid $= 2 \times 882 = ₹\,1764$

Time $= 2$ yr, $r = 5\%$

Using compound interest formula,

$1764 = P\left[1 + \dfrac{5}{100}\right]^2$

$\Rightarrow P = \dfrac{1764}{\left(\dfrac{21}{20}\right)^2} = \dfrac{1764 \times 400}{441} = 1600$

$\therefore$ Amount borrowed was $₹\,1600$.

5. Let the sum of money be $₹\,P$.

According to the question,

$\qquad \dfrac{216}{125}P = P\left(1 + \dfrac{r}{100}\right)^3$

$\Rightarrow \quad \left(\dfrac{6}{5}\right)^3 = \left(1 + \dfrac{r}{100}\right)^3$

$\Rightarrow \quad 1 + \dfrac{r}{100} = \dfrac{6}{5}$

$\Rightarrow \quad r = \dfrac{1}{5} \times 100$

$\therefore \quad r = 20\%$

6. $r = 5\%, T = 2$ yr $\qquad$ [given]

Total amount paid for 2 yr

$\quad = ₹(5000 + 3820) = ₹\,8820, P = ?$

$\therefore \quad 8820 = P\left[1 + \dfrac{5}{100}\right]^2$

$\Rightarrow \quad P = \dfrac{8820}{\left(\dfrac{21}{20}\right)^2}$

$\Rightarrow \quad P = \dfrac{8820 \times 400}{441}$

$\Rightarrow \quad P = ₹\,8000$

8. Interest paid by Mehak

$\qquad = \dfrac{62500 \times 2 \times 4}{100}$

$\qquad = ₹\,5000$

$\qquad [\because P = 62500, r = 2\%, t = 4]$

But, in case of Monisha,

$P = 60000, r = 2\%, t = 4$

$\therefore \quad A = 60000 \times \left(1 + \dfrac{4}{100}\right)^2$

$\qquad = 60000 \times \dfrac{104 \times 104}{10000}$

$\qquad = 64896$

Interest paid $= 64896 - 60000$

$\qquad = 4896$

$\therefore$ Mehak paid more interest by

$\qquad = 5000 - 4896 = ₹\,104$

9. n is the simple interest on m.

p is the simple interest on n.

Let time be t and rate be r.

For both cases (m and n),

$\qquad n = \dfrac{m \times r \times t}{100}$

$\Rightarrow \quad r \times t = \dfrac{100\,n}{m}$

$\Rightarrow \quad \dfrac{r \times t}{100} = \dfrac{n}{m} \qquad \ldots(i)$

Again, $\quad p = \dfrac{n \times r \times t}{100}$

$\Rightarrow \quad \dfrac{r \times t}{100} = \dfrac{p}{n} \qquad \ldots(ii)$

From Eqs. (i) and (ii), we get

$\qquad \dfrac{n}{m} = \dfrac{p}{n}$

$\Rightarrow \qquad n^2 = mp$

10. Difference between CI and SI $= 1800$

$t = 2$ yr

Using formula,

Sum $(P) =$ Difference $\times \left(\dfrac{100}{r}\right)^2$

$\therefore \quad P = 1800 \times \left(\dfrac{100}{r}\right)^2 \qquad \ldots(i)$

Also, SI $= 28800, t = 2$ yr

$\therefore \quad \dfrac{P \times r \times 2}{100} = 28800$

$\Rightarrow P = \dfrac{28800 \times 100}{2r} \qquad \ldots(ii)$

From Eqs. (i) and (ii), we get

$\Rightarrow \quad 1800 \times \dfrac{100}{r} \times \dfrac{100}{r} = \dfrac{28800 \times 100}{2r}$

$\Rightarrow \qquad 288r^2 = 3600r$

$\Rightarrow \quad 144r^2 - 1800r = 0$

$\Rightarrow \quad 36r(4r - 50) = 0$

$\Rightarrow \qquad 4r - 50 = 0$

or $\quad 36r = 0 \Rightarrow r = 0 \quad$ [not possible]

$\therefore \quad r = \dfrac{50}{4} = \dfrac{25}{2}\%$

$\therefore$ $P = 1800 \times \dfrac{100}{\dfrac{25}{2}} \times \dfrac{100}{\dfrac{25}{2}}$

$\qquad = \dfrac{1800 \times 2 \times 100 \times 2 \times 100}{25 \times 25}$

$\qquad = ₹\,115200$

11. Let amount at 5% be $₹\,x$.

$\therefore$ Amount at 8% $= ₹\,(1550 - x)$

In SI case,

$\dfrac{x \times 5 \times 3}{100} + \dfrac{(1550 - x) \times 8 \times 3}{100}$

$\qquad = 300$

$\Rightarrow \quad 15x + 1550 \times 24 - 24x$

$\qquad \qquad = 300 \times 100$

$\Rightarrow \quad 37200 - 30000 = 9x$

$\Rightarrow \qquad 7200 = 9x$

$\Rightarrow \qquad x = 800$

$\therefore$ Amount lent at 5% $= ₹\,800$

Now, amount lent at 8%

$\qquad = ₹(1550 - 800) = 750$

$\therefore$ Required ratio $= \dfrac{800}{750} = 16:15$

Alternate method

Total interest paid $= ₹\,300$

$\qquad \qquad P = ₹\,1550$

$\qquad \qquad T = 3$ yr

$\therefore \quad r = \dfrac{300 \times 100}{1550 \times 3} = \dfrac{200}{31}$

[it is called equated interest rate]

We have,

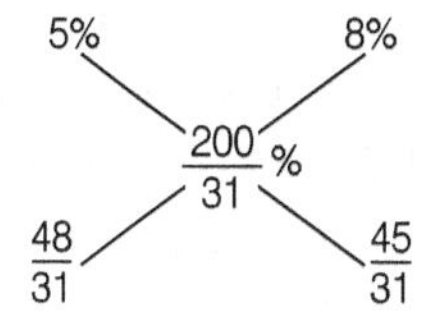

$\therefore$ Required ratio $= \dfrac{48}{31} : \dfrac{45}{31} = 16 : 15$

13. Difference before CI and SI

$\qquad = ₹\,(410 - 400) = ₹\,10$

Use, formula for 2 yr

$r = \dfrac{2 \times \text{Difference in CI and SI}}{SI} \times 100$

$\qquad = \dfrac{2 \times 10}{400} \times 100 = 5\%$

14. Rate for 2 yr $= 6\%$

Rate for next 3 yr $= 9\%$

Rate for beyond 5 yr $= 14\%$

Total amount paid $= ₹\,11400$

Time $= 9$ yr

$P = ?$

$\therefore \quad \dfrac{P \times 6 \times 2}{100} + \dfrac{P \times 3 \times 9}{100}$

$\qquad + \dfrac{P \times 14 \times 4}{100} = 11400$

[$\because r = 6\%$ for 2 yr, 9% from 3 yr, time
left $= 9 - (2 + 3) = 4$yr, $r = 14\%$]

$$\Rightarrow 12P + 27P + 56P = 11400 \times 100$$
$$\Rightarrow 95P = 11400 \times 100$$
$$\Rightarrow P = \frac{11400 \times 100}{95}$$
$$\therefore \qquad P = ₹\ 12000$$

15. Karishma invested, after 2 yr
$$= ₹\ 9680$$
Karishma invested, after 3 yr
$$= ₹\ 10648$$
$$\therefore \quad \frac{10648}{9680} = \frac{P\left(1 + \dfrac{r}{100}\right)^3}{P\left(1 + \dfrac{r}{100}\right)^2}$$
$$\Rightarrow \quad 1 + \frac{r}{100} = \frac{10648}{9680}$$

16.
$$\Rightarrow \quad r = \frac{10648 - 9680}{9680} \times 100$$
$$\Rightarrow \quad r = \frac{968}{9680} \times 100 = 10\%$$

16. Population of village = 8000
Increase in first year = 10%
i.e. population after 1 yr,
$$8000 + 8000 \times \frac{10}{100} = 8800$$
20% increase in second year
i.e. population after 2 yr,
$$8800 + 8800 \times \frac{20}{100} = 10560$$
Due to malaria, it decreases by 20% in 3rd yr.
∴ Population after 3 yr
$$= 10560 - 10560 \times \frac{20}{100}$$
$$= 10560 - 2112 = 8448$$

Alternate method
r for Ist year = 10%
r for IInd year = 20%
r for IIIrd year = 20%
∴ After 3 yr, population will be
$$A = 8000\left(1 + \frac{10}{100}\right)\left(1 + \frac{20}{100}\right)\left(1 - \frac{20}{100}\right)$$
$$= 8000 \times \frac{11}{10} \times \frac{12}{10} \times \frac{8}{10} = 8448$$

17. I. False II. False
III. True IV. True
V. True

18. I. 1655.06 II. 2.5%
III. ₹ 1000 IV. 4
V. >

10 · *Direct and Inverse Proportion*

1. Direct proportion
$$x \propto y$$
$$x = Ky \quad [K \text{ is a constant}]$$
$$\therefore \quad \frac{x}{y} = K$$

2. $x = 10, y = 25$
$$\Rightarrow \quad \frac{y}{x} = \frac{25}{10} = \frac{5}{2}$$

3. $v = 5, u = 15$
$$u \times v = 15 \times 5 = 75$$
$$[\text{inverse proportion, } xy = K]$$

4. Diesel consumed = 54 L
Distance covered = 297 km
$$\therefore \quad \text{Distance/litre} = \frac{297}{54} \text{ km} = \frac{11}{2}$$
Distance = 550 km
$$\therefore \text{ Diesel consumed} = 550 \div \frac{11}{2}$$
$$= 100\,\text{L}$$
∴ Diesel required = 100 L – 54 L
$$= 46\,\text{L}$$

5. Since, the price and quantity are directly proportional.
$$\therefore \quad \frac{3}{105} = \frac{2}{x} \Rightarrow x = 70$$
and
$$\frac{3}{105} = \frac{y}{210}$$
$$\Rightarrow \quad y = 6$$

6. Five years ago, the ratio of son's and his mother's age = 2 : 5
Let x be proportionality constant.
i.e. age of son = $2x$
and age of mother = $5x$
After 5 yr, age of son = $(2x + 5) + 5$
Age of mother = $(5x + 5) + 5$

According to the question,
$$\frac{2x + 10}{5x + 10} = \frac{4}{7}$$
$$\Rightarrow \quad 14x + 70 = 20x + 40$$
$$\Rightarrow \quad 6x = 30 \Rightarrow x = 5$$
∴ Present age of son
$$= 2x + 5 = 2 \times 5 + 5 = 15 \text{ yr}$$

7. $x_1 = 6, y_1 = 4$
$$\Rightarrow \quad \frac{x_1}{y_1} = \frac{6}{4} = \frac{3}{2}$$
and $x_2 = 12, y_2 = 8$
$$\Rightarrow \quad \frac{x_2}{y_2} = \frac{12}{8} = \frac{3}{2}$$
i.e. $\dfrac{x_3}{y_3} = \dfrac{3}{2} = K... \qquad$ [fixed]
$$\frac{x_1}{y_1} = \frac{x_2}{y_2} = ... = K$$
i.e. increase in $x \propto$ increase in y
Hence, $x \propto y$

8. Total men = 100
Food available for 24 days.
Added persons = 20
∴ Total available persons = 100 + 20
$$= 120$$
∴ Days for which food will last
$$= \frac{24 \times 100}{120} = 20$$

9. Amount = ₹ 5000
Interest = ₹ 1000
Time = 3 yr
New amount = ₹ 30000
∴ Interest = ?
Since, the amount and interest are directly proportional.
$$\therefore \quad \frac{5000}{1000} = \frac{30000}{x}$$
$$\Rightarrow \quad x = 6000$$

11. Total time of schooling
$$= 30 \times 8 = 240 \text{ min}$$
Now, total number of periods = 10
∴ Duration of each period
$$= \frac{240}{10} \text{ min}$$
$$= 24\,\text{min}$$
[since, they are inversely proportional]

12. Number of men working originally
$$= 300$$
Number of hours working
$$= 60\,\text{per week}$$
New number of hours of working
$$= 40\,\text{per week}$$
Let number of men working after change in working hours be x.
Since, they are inversely proportional.
$$\therefore \quad 300 \times 60 = 40 \times x$$
$$\Rightarrow \quad \frac{300 \times 60}{40} = x$$
$$\Rightarrow \quad x = 450$$

13. Original typing speed of Michael
$$= 30\,\text{words per minute}$$
Time taken to finish the essay = 2 h
Let the new speed be x words per minute.
New time required to type the essay
$$= 1.5\,\text{h}$$
Since, they are inversely proportional.
$$\therefore 30 \times 2 = 1.5x \Rightarrow x = \frac{30 \times 2}{1.5}$$
$$= 40 \text{ words per minute}$$

14. Number of fans = 50
Cost of fans = ₹ 50 × 500 = ₹25000
New cost of each fan = ₹(500 + 20)
$$= ₹520$$
∴ Number of fans in that amount
$$= \frac{25000}{520} \approx 48$$
[since, they are inversely proportional]

Mᴀᴛʜᴇᴍᴀᴛɪᴄs **Oʟʏᴍᴘɪᴀᴅ** Cʟᴀss VIII

15. Cost of 2 watches = Cost of 3 fans
$$= ₹ 1500$$
$$2 \text{ watches} = 3 \text{ fans}$$
$$\Rightarrow \quad 1 \text{ watch} = \frac{3}{2} \text{ fans}$$
$$\Rightarrow \quad 6 \text{ watches} = \frac{6 \times 3}{2} \text{ fans}$$
$$= 9 \text{ fans}$$
∴ Total number of fans
$$(6 \text{ fans} + 6 \text{ watches})$$
$$= 6 + 9 = 15 \text{ fans}$$
∴ Total cost $$= ₹ \frac{1500}{3} \times 15$$
$$= ₹ 7500$$

16. I. False   II. True
    III. True   IV. True

17. I. directly proportional
    II. decreases
    III. 8:15
    IV. no variation
    V. 12:1

18. 8 persons = 6 days
    1 person = 6×8 days
    ∴ 6 persons $= \dfrac{6 \times 8}{6}$ days
$$= 8 \text{ days}$$

20. In 1 day, the number of cows graze the field $= 60 \times 15$

    In 10 days, the number of cows graze the field
$$= \frac{60}{10} \times 15 = 90$$
    [since, they are inversely proportional]

21. Average speed while going to school
$$= 12 \text{ km/h}$$
    Time taken to reach school = 20 min
    ∴ Speed needed to reach school in
$$15 \text{ min} = \frac{12 \times 20}{15}$$
$$= 16 \text{ km/h}$$

22. $\dfrac{\text{Men}}{\text{Time}} = \dfrac{5}{20} = \dfrac{1}{4}$
    Men $\times$ Time $= 5 \times 20 = 100$
$$20 \times 5 = 100$$
$$10 \times 10 = 100$$

$$\vdots \quad \vdots \quad \vdots$$
$$50 \times 2 = 100$$
It is of the form $xy = K$.
$$\therefore \quad \frac{100}{20} = 5, \ \frac{100}{4} = 25$$

23. 30 km distance covered in 30 min.
    ∴ 15 km distance covered in
$$\frac{30}{30} \times 15 = 15 \text{ min} = \frac{15}{60} \text{ h} = \frac{1}{4} \text{ h}$$

24. $\dfrac{5}{8}$ work is done in 10 days.

    1 work is to be done in $10 \times \dfrac{8}{5} = 16$ days.
$$\therefore \quad \frac{3}{4} \text{ work} = \frac{16 \times 3}{4} = 12 \text{ days}$$
    ∴ Number of extra days $= 12 - 10$
$$= 2$$

25. Since, they are inversely proportional.
$$\therefore \frac{\frac{4}{5}}{1} = \frac{20}{x} \Rightarrow x = 25 \text{ min}$$

26. 3 pages containing 25 lines in each page.
    ∴ Total number of lines $= 25 \times 3$
$$= 75$$
$$\text{Time taken} = 2 \text{ h}$$
    Now, 5 pages of 30 lines each.
    ∴ Total number of lines $= 30 \times 5$
$$= 150$$
    ∴ Time taken $= \dfrac{150}{75} \times 2 \text{ h} = 4 \text{ h}$

27. 10 men can do a work in 6 days.
    So, 1 man can do the same work in 10×6 days.
    ∴ 8 men can do the same work in $\dfrac{10 \times 6}{8}$ days.

    Also, 15 women can do the same work in 6 days.
    So, 1 woman can do the same work in 15×6 days.
    3 women can do the same work in $\dfrac{15 \times 6}{3}$ days.

    If 8 men and 3 women together do the same work, then they will complete the part of it in 1 day
$$= \frac{1}{\frac{60}{8}} + \frac{1}{\frac{90}{3}}$$

$$= \frac{8}{60} + \frac{3}{90}$$
$$= \frac{2}{15} + \frac{1}{30} = \frac{4+1}{30} = \frac{5}{30}$$
$$= \frac{1}{6} \text{ part}$$
So, 8 men and 3 women together complete work in 6 days.

Alternative method
10 men = 15 women
[both complete in same number of days]
$$\therefore \quad 1 \text{ man} = \frac{15}{10} \text{ women} = \frac{3}{2}$$
    ∴ 8 men + 3 women
$$= \left(8 \times \frac{3}{2} + 3 \right) \text{ women}$$
$$= 15 \text{ women}$$
    ∴ 15 women can do in 6 days.

28. First pipe can fill tank in 30 min.
    ∴ It fills in 1 min $= \dfrac{1}{30}$ tank

    Similarly, for second pipe, in 1 min
$$= \frac{1}{40} \text{ tank}$$
    Empty pipe, in 1 m $= \dfrac{1}{20}$ tank

    Tank filled in 1 min by all pipes
$$= \frac{1}{30} + \frac{1}{40} - \frac{1}{20}$$
$$= \frac{4 + 3 - 6}{120} = \frac{1}{120}$$
    ∴ Time taken to fill the tank
$$= 120 \text{ min}$$
$$\therefore \frac{1}{2} \text{ tank} = \frac{1}{2} \times 120 = 60 \text{ min} = 1 \text{ h}$$

29. Length of train = 200 m
    Time taken in crossing the pole
$$= 10 \text{ min}$$
    ∴ Distance covered
$$= \text{Length of train} = 200 \text{ m}$$
    ∴ Time taken to cross the man
$$= 10 \text{ min}$$

30. I. False   II. True   III. False
    IV. True

31. I. $12\dfrac{1}{2}$ II. 100
    III. 2   IV. 250

ANSWERS AND EXPLANATIONS

4. $\angle A + \angle D = 180°$ [since, $AB \| CD$]

$\Rightarrow \angle D = 180° - 55°$

     [$\because \angle A = 55°$ given]

$= 125°$

5. Using property, sum of all exterior angles of a polygon is 360°.

6. $\because$ Sum of adjacent angles of a parallelogram = 180°

$\therefore \quad 7x + 2x = 180°$

$\Rightarrow \quad\quad 9x = 180°$

$\Rightarrow \quad\quad x = 20°$

Hence, angles are 140°, 40°, 140°, 40°.

7.

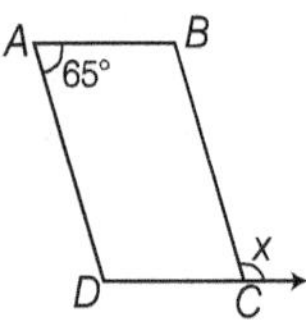

$\because$ Opposite angles of a parallelogram are equal.

$\angle A = \angle C = 65°$

$\therefore \quad \angle x = 180° - 65° = 115°$

     [by linear pair]

8. Sum of adjacent angles = 180°

$\therefore \ x + 40° + x - 20° = 180°$

$\Rightarrow 2x = 160° \Rightarrow x = 80°$

So, angles are 120° and 60°.

9. $\because$ Sum of all angles of a quadrilateral

$= 360°$

Two angles = 60° and 40°   [given]

$\therefore$ Sum of rest of the two angles

$= 360° - (60° + 40°) = 260°$

According to the question,

$16x + 10x = 260°$

$\Rightarrow \quad\quad 26x = 260°$

$\Rightarrow \quad\quad x = 10°$

So, angles are 160° and 100°.

10. $\because$ Sum of angles of a quadrilateral

$= 360°$

$\therefore \quad\quad x + 2x + 3x + 4x = 360°$

$\Rightarrow \quad\quad 10x = 360°$

$\Rightarrow \quad\quad x = 36°$

$\therefore$ Greatest angle $= 4 \times 36° = 144°$

11. $\because$ Sum of adjacent angles = 180°

$\therefore (2x - 4)° + (3x - 1)° = 180°$

$\Rightarrow \quad\quad 5x = 185°$

$\Rightarrow \quad\quad x = 37°$

$\therefore$ Angles are $(37 \times 2 - 4), (37 \times 3 - 1)$.

$= 37 \times 2 - 4, 37 \times 3 - 1$

$= 70°, 110°, 70°, 110°$

13. According to the property of rectangle,

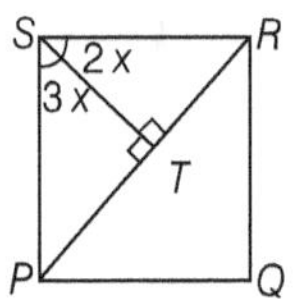

$3x + 2x = 90°$

$\Rightarrow \quad 5x = 90°$

$\Rightarrow \quad x = 18°$

$\therefore \quad\quad 3x = 54°$ and $2x = 36°$

In $\triangle PTS$,

$54° + 90° + \angle TPS = 180°$

   [$\because$ sum of angles of triangle = 180°]

$\Rightarrow \quad\quad \angle TPS = 36°$

$\therefore \angle TPQ = 90° - 36° = 54°$

14.

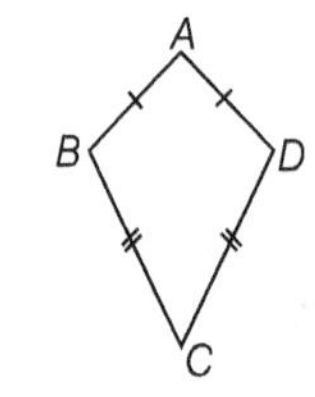

Given,

Perimeter of playground = 106 m

One side = 23 m

Let $\quad\quad AB = 23$ m

$\therefore \quad AB = AD = 23$ m

Also, $\quad\quad BC = CD$

$\Rightarrow BC + CD = 106 - (23 + 23)$

$= 60$ m

$\Rightarrow \quad 2BC = 60$. [$\because BC = CD$]

$\therefore \quad\quad BC = 30$ m

15. Given,

$\angle S = \angle Q, \angle P = \angle R$

$\angle Q = 180° - 60° = 120°$

   [$\because \angle PQR + \angle RQY = 180°$]

$\therefore \quad\quad \angle S = \angle Q = 120°$

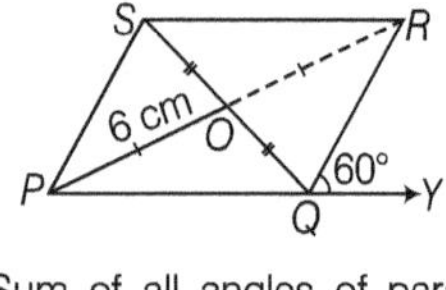

$\because$ Sum of all angles of parallelogram $PQRS = 360°$

$\therefore \ \angle P + \angle R = 360° - 2 \times 120°$

$= 120°$

$2\angle P = 120° \Rightarrow \angle P = 60° = \angle R$

$\therefore \angle S : \angle R = 120° : 60° = 2 : 1$

16. Sum of all interior angles of a hexagon of side $n = (n - 2) \times 180°$

Here, $\quad\quad n = 6$

$(6 - 2) \times 180° = 720°$

Now,

$x + (x - 5) + (x - 5) + (2x - 5)$

$+ (2x - 5) + (2x + 20) = 720°$

$\Rightarrow \quad\quad 9x = 720°$

$\therefore \quad\quad x = 80°$

17. I. False   II. True   III. True

IV. True   V. True

18. I. 60°   II. Square   III. 10   IV. 90°   V. 6 cm

www.ingramcontent.com/pod-product-compliance
Lightning Source LLC
LaVergne TN
LVHW080549200726
843510LV00008B/1060